THE BOOK OF
INGENIOUSLY
DARING
CHEMISTRY

★ ★

SEAN CONNOLLY

★ ★

WORKMAN PUBLISHING · NEW YORK

Library of Congress Cataloging-in-Publication Data is available.

ISBN 978-0-7611-8010-4

Cover and interior illustrations by Cara Bean
Design by Gordon Whiteside and Nina Simoneaux
Editing by Danny Cooper
Production editing by Beth Levy
Production manager Steven Bucsok
Photo research by Ken Yu

Photo Credits: **Adobe Stock**: akepong p. 138; apttone p. 33; Bergamont p. 70;
BillionPhotos.com p. 91; boonchuay1970 p. 33; Antonio Gravante p. 197; JPS
p. 122; Jultud p. 46; Audrius Merfeldas p. 176; Pixelrobot pp. 88, 203; SimFan
p. 125; Sommai p. 167; Diana Taliun p. 166; Björn Wylezich p. 33. **Alamy
Images**: OJO Images Ltd. p. 56; RTimages p. 71; Konstantin Shaklein p. 115;
Stephen Saks Photography p. 102; Andrzej Tokarski p. 81; World History Archive
p. 113; Björn Wylezich p. 105. **Dreamstime**: Nilsz p. 73. **Getty Images**: Apic/
RETIRED/Hulton Archive p. 137; Bettmann p. 4; Andy Crawford/Dorling
Kindersley p. 113; De Agostini Picture Library p. 193; DEA PICTURE LIBRARY/
De Agostini p. 139; Heritage Images/Hulton Archive p. 149; HomePixel/iStock
p. 81; hudiemm/iStock p. 13; JMLPYT/iStock p. 195; Sebastian Kaulitzki/
Science Photo Library p. 168; Dorling Kindersley p. 136; Leemage/Universal
Images Group p. 54; Martin Leigh/Oxford Scientific p. 177; Lidara/iStock p. 57;
mashuk/DigitalVision Vectors p. 22; pepifoto/E+ p. 123; Athit Perawongmetha/
Moment p. 42; Photo 12/Universal Images Group p. 176; PHOTOS.com p. 69;
Science & Society Picture Library/SSPL p. 185; showcake/iStock p. 44; Fernando
Takashi Silva/Moment p. 186; Wavebreakmedia/iStock p. 123; Toyohiro Yamada/
The Image Bank p. 147.

Workman books are available at special discounts when purchased
in bulk for premiums and sales promotions as well as for fund-raising
or educational use. Special editions or book excerpts can also be created
to specification. For details, contact the Special Sales Director at
the address below, or send an email to specialmarkets@workman.com.

Workman Publishing Co., Inc.
225 Varick Street
New York, NY 10014-4381
workman.com

WORKMAN is a registered trademark of Workman Publishing Co., Inc.

Printed in the United States of America
First printing July 2018

10 9 8 7 6 5 4 3 2 1

★ ★

*To my wife, Frederika, and
our own special chemisty.*

★ ★

In 1675, Sir Isaac Newton—already celebrated as a scientific genius in his own lifetime—modestly wrote, "If I have seen further it is by standing on the shoulders of Giants." He was referring to the pioneering work of scientists in the preceding centuries, and how he built on their knowledge and discoveries to produce his own scientific contributions.

Well, as you read the following pages you'll join me in standing on Newton's shoulders and quite a few more, besides—the broad shoulders of Galileo, Grace Flyer, Paracelsus, Robert Boyle, Madame Curie, Joseph Priestly, and Dmitri Mendeleev, to name just a few. Some of them devoted their entire lives to science; others gave up their lives for the same cause.

Luckily, those who helped guide this particular book into your hands are still with us, and they deserve my gratitude for their guidance and patience. They include my agent, Jim Levine of the Levine Greenberg Rostan Literary Agency, Workman editor and "brother in arms," Danny Cooper, and the Workman team responsible for helping my words take shape on the page— production editor Beth Levy, production manager Steven Bucsok, typesetter Barbara Peragine, designer Gordon Whiteside, and illustrator Cara Bean.

The following individuals and organizations have also played a part in producing this book, either through direct consultation or providing yet more "shoulders" for me to stand on: The Bath Royal Literary and Scientific Institution, Berkshire Film & Video, Frank Ciccotti, Gregory Etter, Dr. Gary Hoffman, Dr. Peter Lydon, MIT's Educational Studies Program, Peter Rielly, Elizabeth Stell, Williams College Astronomy Department, and Woods Hole Oceanographic Institution.

CONTENTS

CHAPTER 20

TIN

THE "DIRTY DOZEN"

INTRODUCTION

MATTER REALLY MATTERS

Think about that word "matter" for a moment. Do you have any idea what it means? Is everything some sort of matter? Or maybe some stuff is and other stuff is something else? Or could it be that things are made up partly of matter, with other things, like forces, mixed in? Maybe none of these answers is even close? Or the answer is just too darned complicated to find? *Does it even really matter?*

The answer is 100 percent YES. It does matter, and best of all, finding out how and why is a whole lot of fun. That's what this book will do. It's going to show you how every-

thing *is* matter, but more than that, it will help you see the world around you in a whole new way. You'll under-stand why things look the way they do (or why they sometimes can't be seen), why they behave the way they do, and what can and cannot be changed about them.

The following pages will take you on a chemistry journey through the inner workings of all matter. When we think of matter, we think of "things"—doughnuts, car tires, cell phones, and pineapples. They all seem dif-ferent, but if we look more closely, we learn that those familiar examples share certain elements; it's just that those elements are put together in different ways.

And it's that word, "elements," that is the key to understanding matter. Once you start separating the bits that make an apple an apple or a pencil a pencil, you eventually get to a point where you can't do any more separating. You find the basic building blocks of matter, the things that can be arranged in all sorts of awesome ways to make the world around us. These are the elements, the "end of the line," beyond which it's impossible to reduce things into simpler structures.

That is the world this book inhabits—the world of elements. You'll see that these elements are all atoms, but atoms differ from one another in particular ways. The differences come from the tiny particles that all atoms have, but in different numbers and arrangements. The number of protons (the positively charged particles) is the main "ID check" of an element. The protons are all in the nucleus, or center, of each atom. And just to make things interesting, you might also find neutrons inside some of these atoms, too. Neutrons have no charge, but they do have mass (weight) . . . and that can make elements behave differently.

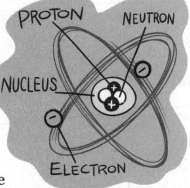

Things really get going when you come across the negatively charged electrons, which orbit the nucleus a little bit like planets orbiting the Sun. Just as you might have noticed with electricity or magnets, opposites attract, so the negative charge of one element might attract the positive charge of another . . . leading to some pretty cool connections. Electrons are the fidgety members of the element drama—they might stay put and attract other elements, or jump off to a different element, or even share time between two elements. At this point, you come to learn one of the keys to all science: The behavior of electrons dictates so much of what we call chemistry.

SETTING THE TABLE

Just how do those elements get along with each other? It's easy to see that gold looks different from carbon and each of those is unlike aluminum or oxygen. What's harder to see is that the elements aren't all out in the world behaving uncontrollably—unlike your screwball brother or sister, there's a way to predict their behavior. How? That's where the periodic table of elements comes into play.

The periodic table is a road map of all the matter in the universe. It arranges the elements according to the particles that make them up. Since the main ID for an element is its number of protons, the table begins with hydrogen (which has one proton, so its atomic number is 1) and ends with oganesson, which has an atomic number of 118. You probably hadn't ever heard of oganesson before a few seconds ago, but now you can probably work out how many protons it has!

We've gone pretty easily from 1 to 118, but why are the elements arranged in rows and columns? That takes us back to those orbiting electrons. Think again of electron orbits, which scientists call "shells" or "energy levels." Well, atoms have seven possible electron shells. Once the innermost shell (which can hold two electrons) has been filled up, electrons move to the second shell, and when that's filled, they start in on the third, and so forth. And each shell can hold more electrons than the previous one. But take another look at the periodic table. Notice how that bigger top chunk has seven rows—that's because there are seven possible electron shells. So the elements in the first row have one electron shell, those in the second have two, and so on, right up to the seventh row.

THE PERIODIC TABLE OF ELEMENTS

PERIODS

1 H																	2 He
3 Li	4 Be											5 B	6 C	7 N	8 O	9 F	10 Ne
11 Na	12 Mg											13 Al	14 Si	15 P	16 S	17 Cl	18 Ar
19 K	20 Ca	21 Sc	22 Ti	23 V	24 Cr	25 Mn	26 Fe	27 Co	28 Ni	29 Cu	30 Zn	31 Ga	32 Ge	33 As	34 Se	35 Br	36 Kr
37 Rb	38 Sr	39 Y	40 Zr	41 Nb	42 Mo	43 Tc	44 Ru	45 Rh	46 Pd	47 Ag	48 Cd	49 In	50 Sn	51 Sb	52 Te	53 I	54 Xe
55 Cs	56 Ba		72 Hf	73 Ta	74 W	75 Re	76 Os	77 Ir	78 Pt	79 Au	80 Hg	81 Tl	82 Pb	83 Bi	84 Po	85 At	86 Rn
87 Fr	88 Ra		104 Rf	105 Db	106 Sg	107 Bh	108 Hs	109 Mt	110 Ds	111 Rg	112 Cn	113 Nh	114 Fl	115 Mc	116 Lv	117 Ts	118 Og

57 La	58 Ce	59 Pr	60 Nd	61 Pm	62 Sm	63 Eu	64 Gd	65 Tb	66 Dy	67 Ho	68 Er	69 Tm	70 Yb	71 Lu
89 Ac	90 Th	91 Pa	92 U	93 Np	94 Pu	95 Am	96 Cm	97 Bk	98 Cf	99 Es	100 Fm	101 Md	102 No	103 Lr

GROUPS

When scientists first grouped elements in this way, they called each row a "period." So they were building a "periodic table." Ta-da! This is all beginning to fall into place. But what about the columns? What do they mean?

The answer is still all about electrons—specifically, the number of electrons in the outermost shell of each element. The electrons in the inner shells are tucked away from contact with other atoms, but those in the outer shells (called "valence electrons") can jump ship, invite others, or split their time with another element. As long as they haven't filled up all the available spaces in that shell, that is. Those filled shells don't deal with other elements, just like the electrons of the inner shells.

We know that the rows tell us how many electron shells an element has. The columns go further, telling us how many electrons are in those outer shells. Look down the first column, starting with hydrogen. Even though the elements in that column pile on more and more electrons as you go farther down, they all have one thing in common: Each of them has just one electron in its outer shell. Chemists call a group of elements making up one of these columns—guess what—a "group."

And in the next column? Each member of that group of elements—containing some familiar names (magnesium, calcium) and some unfamiliar (beryllium, strontium)—has two electrons in that outer shell.

Columns 3 to 12 are the "rebels" of the periodic table. They have valence electrons in every electron shell, not just the outermost shell. That gives them some unusual properties, which we'll examine firsthand later in the book. Columns 13 onward get back in step, though: From boron on down, the elements have three valence electrons, carbon's column has four, nitrogen's column has five, and so on.

HOW THIS BOOK WORKS

This book will take you on a trip through the periodic table. Not all of it, because many of the elements—especially in the smaller bottom chunk—are rare, dangerous, or exist only for a split second. But you'll be making stops down the rows and across the columns, getting to know enough of the "key players" to see the wider picture. Plus, you'll be able to see how some of the "relatives" of those elements might be extremely dangerous or volatile, even though they share some of the same characteristics.

Each chapter will be devoted to a single element, which you'll get to know really well. The chapter includes that element's:

- Atomic number (how many protons it has)

- Atomic weight (protons plus neutrons, on average)

- Element symbol (the official abbreviation)

- Electrons in the outer shell (also called "valence electrons")

- Melting point (the temperature that makes it melt)

- Boiling point (the temperature that makes it boil)

All of this information defines the essence of an element. You'll also learn more so you can form a clearer picture of that element—what it looks like, when it was discovered, where it is found, the useful stuff it does, and the quirky qualities that help give it character.

Getting to know an element is like being introduced to a new friend, and then it's time to "Meet the Relatives." You'll learn about an element's crazy cousin or wacky uncle, and you'll see how these other elements in their period or group behave, working with similar amounts or arrangements of particles. It's also a chance to find out that some of the wilder chemical reactions—way beyond the scope of "hands-on" experiments—still depend on the same basic chemical ingredients as these familiar elements.

Each of the first 20 chapters of the book focuses on an element that you can find easily—although it's usually combined with one or more other elements. But don't forget: Some of these more familiar elements can still turn out to be dangerous, as you'll see in the "Danger Level" panel.

These chapters will finish with at least one hands-on chemistry experiment to drive home some of the memorable features of the chapter's element. It might involve just the one element, or maybe you'll be getting really scientific by forming compounds (see page 22) with more than one element. Either way it will be fun, and you won't have to worry about getting "scientific material" from special suppliers—you probably have what you need to reveal the mysteries of the periodic table in your kitchen or tucked away in a closet.

After rolling up your sleeves with those 20 elements, you'll learn about the "Dirty Dozen"—12 of the most dangerous elements of all. Some of these, like plutonium, have the potential to blow the world to bits. Others, such as polonium, could poison an entire city in an instant. You'll also learn about elements that people once thought were safe, or even healthful. Now they know better!

It's time to start exploring.

ATOMIC NUMBER: 1	ELECTRONS IN OUTERMOST SHELL: 1
ATOMIC WEIGHT: 1.0079	MELTING POINT: -434.81°F (-259.34°C)
ELEMENT SYMBOL: H	BOILING POINT: -423.18°F (-252.88°C)

CHAPTER 1

HYDROGEN

H																	He
Li	Be											B	C	N	O	F	Ne
Na	Mg											Al	Si	P	S	Cl	Ar
K	Ca	Sc	Ti	V	Cr	Mn	Fe	Co	Ni	Cu	Zn	Ga	Ge	As	Se	Br	Kr
Rb	Sr	Y	Zr	Nb	Mo	Tc	Ru	Rh	Pd	Ag	Cd	In	Sn	Sb	Te	I	Xe
Cs	Ba		Hf	Ta	W	Re	Os	Ir	Pt	Au	Hg	Tl	Pb	Bi	Po	At	Rn
Fr	Ra		Rf	Db	Sg	Bh	Hs	Mt	Ds	Rg	Cn	Nh	Fl	Mc	Lv	Ts	Og

La	Ce	Pr	Nd	Pm	Sm	Eu	Gd	Tb	Dy	Ho	Er	Tm	Yb	Lu
Ac	Th	Pa	U	Np	Pu	Am	Cm	Bk	Cf	Es	Fm	Md	No	Lr

"**W**e're number one! We're number one!"

OK, it's hard to imagine a bunch of hydrogen atoms shouting like a rowdy crowd at a college basketball game . . . but they'd certainly have the right to boast a little. Hydrogen is number one on the periodic table because it's the lightest element, with just one proton (positively charged particle) in its nucleus. But it is also the most abundant element in the universe and one of the first three elements—along with helium and lithium—that were created in the Big Bang almost 14 billion years ago (see page 14). And because it combines easily with other elements, it forms part of every living thing on the planet. Hey, not bad!

WHAT DOES HYDROGEN LOOK LIKE?

You wouldn't notice hydrogen unless the thermometer hovered a few hundred degrees below zero. At those frosty temperatures you would find either liquid hydrogen or—just a few degrees colder still—frozen hydrogen. But at normal temperatures, hydrogen is a gas, and it's colorless and odorless.

STATES OF MATTER

All matter exists in one form—called a state—or another. Scientists describe them as "observable states," because they are the forms that we can see. The four observable states of matter are solid, liquid, gas, and plasma (a special type of gas). Matter can change state when it is affected by a change in temperature, pressure, or electric charge. Just think of ice (a solid) melting to become water (a liquid) and then boiling to become water vapor (a gas). The gas inside a fluorescent light becomes a plasma when an electric charge passes through it.

WHEN WAS HYDROGEN DISCOVERED?

A couple of scientists in the 16th and 17th centuries were really close to discovering hydrogen. Meaning that they produced it but didn't realize that they were observing a new element. The Swiss scientist known as Paracelsus (full name Philippus Aureolus Theophrastus Bombastus von Hohenheim) and Irish chemist Robert Boyle both noticed something when they dropped metals into strong acids: The bubbles that were produced would ignite if a flame touched them.

It was an Englishman, Henry Cavendish, who recognized that these flammable bubbles were, in fact, a separate element altogether. He also noticed that "dew" (soon to be identified as water) was produced when the element burned. We now know that's because the hydrogen uses oxygen in the air to burn . . . and one of the results is water (H_2O).

Cavendish decided those bubbles were full of "inflammable air," but that doesn't sound enough like an element. It took the French scientist Antoine Lavoisier in 1783 to make up the name that stuck: hydrogen, meaning "water producer."

Henry Cavendish

WHERE IS HYDROGEN USED?

Hydrogen is everywhere, and that's no exaggeration. Being the basis of all life is a good start—hydrogen is an important part of the DNA molecule, which contains the genetic instructions for the growth and development of living organisms. Tying in hydrogen with oxygen produces water, of course—and there sure is plenty of *that* on planet Earth.

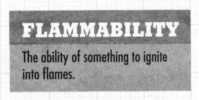

FLAMMABILITY

The ability of something to ignite into flames.

The list of hydrogen's applications could almost fill this book! It's used in food production, fertilizers, electricity production, electronics, and even rocket fuel. The lightness of hydrogen, coupled with its low cost, led engineers to fill huge airships (called zeppelins or blimps) with it at the beginning of the 20th century. Unfortunately, hydrogen's other important feature—flammability—stopped that trend in its tracks. In 1937,

the German airship *Hindenburg* exploded in dramatic fashion as it passed over New Jersey, killing 35 people.

Things might be looking up again for hydrogen's link with transportation, though. Many people view it as a pollution-free alternative to dirty fossil fuels (such as gasoline and diesel). Maybe hydrogen-powered cars will be common by the second half of the 21st century.

Meet the Relatives 🤝 He

THE LONELY PAIR

1 H																	2 He
3 Li	4 Be											5 B	6 C	7 N	8 O	9 F	10 Ne
11 Na	12 Mg											13 Al	14 Si	15 P	16 S	17 Cl	18 Ar
19 K	20 Ca	21 Sc	22 Ti	23 V	24 Cr	25 Mn	26 Fe	27 Co	28 Ni	29 Cu	30 Zn	31 Ga	32 Ge	33 As	34 Se	35 Br	36 Kr
37 Rb	38 Sr	39 Y	40 Zr	41 Nb	42 Mo	43 Tc	44 Ru	45 Rh	46 Pd	47 Ag	48 Cd	49 In	50 Sn	51 Sb	52 Te	53 I	54 Xe
55 Cs	56 Ba		72 Hf	73 Ta	74 W	75 Re	76 Os	77 Ir	78 Pt	79 Au	80 Hg	81 Tl	82 Pb	83 Bi	84 Po	85 At	86 Rn
87 Fr	88 Ra		104 Rf	105 Db	106 Sg	107 Bh	108 Hs	109 Mt	110 Ds	111 Rg	112 Cn	113 Nh	114 Fl	115 Mc	116 Lv	117 Ts	118 Og

57 La	58 Ce	59 Pr	60 Nd	61 Pm	62 Sm	63 Eu	64 Gd	65 Tb	66 Dy	67 Ho	68 Er	69 Tm	70 Yb	71 Lu
89 Ac	90 Th	91 Pa	92 U	93 Np	94 Pu	95 Am	96 Cm	97 Bk	98 Cf	99 Es	100 Fm	101 Md	102 No	103 Lr

Hydrogen's position on the top-left corner of the periodic table tells us two things. First, we know hydrogen has one electron shell—that's what it means to be in the top row, or period. And being in the farthest-left column, or group, tells us that hydrogen has just one electron in its shell. That means that other elements in the same column, including lithium (Li) and potassium (Na), have just one electron in their outside shell.

But there's a huge gap between hydrogen and its counterpart on the top-right corner of the table—helium (He), the subject of the next chapter. In fact, these two elements are the "odd ones out" in some ways. Other elements have more electron shells, and those shells can contain more and more electrons as you move down the rows.

But—and this is a big but—those other elements try to gain or lose electrons in their outer shell to hit the number eight. That's when they are most settled and stable. If they have six electrons, they'll find an element that can share or give away two electrons. Or, if they have three, they'll probably look for an element with five electrons. Chemists call this the octet rule: Remember that an octet, in science, just like in music, has eight members.

Hydrogen has company up there—right? We're talking about helium again, the only other element in the top row. Like hydrogen, helium has only one electron shell. But what's with the big jump across all those columns from hydrogen to get there? Aha!—you'll only find out by reading about helium in the next chapter.

DANGER LEVEL

Luckily, you won't be experimenting with real hydrogen, which is extremely flammable, but take care on your "long walk" that you don't bump into anything—or anyone!

EXPERIMENT *with the* ELEMENT

Although the distances between the particles making up atoms are very, very small, those same distances are actually very, very big if you imagine viewing everything at a microscopic level. Just to give you an idea: The total volume (amount of space it fills) of an atom is more than a trillion times greater than the volume of the atom's nucleus, yet almost all of the atom's mass is concentrated in that same nucleus. This experiment gives you the chance to picture those distances: You're "going big" to "imagine small."

GET TO KNOW AN ATOM

This experiment is a great way to get to know the relative size of atoms and the bits that make them up. Start with the simplest element, hydrogen, with its one proton and one electron. Hydrogen's single electron isn't in an exact orbit around the nucleus, like that of the Moon orbiting Earth, but we can get an idea of its average distance from the center. You'll be demonstrating that on a waaaay larger scale in the following experiment. Be warned: You'll need to walk a long course, so you should do it in a park or along a sidewalk where you won't get bumped around.

YOU WILL NEED

- ◆ **Pin (with small but noticeable pinhead)**
- ◆ **Small piece of soap**
- ◆ **Tape measure or ruler**
- ◆ **Scissors**
- ◆ **String**
- ◆ **Chalk**

METHOD

1 Stick the pin in the soap and place the soap on the ground. Imagine that it is the nucleus of the hydrogen atom (with its single proton).

2 Use the tape measure and scissors to cut off a 10-foot (3 m) length of string.

3 Starting at the pin, mark out 16 lengths of string, end to end. Use chalk to mark each 10-foot (3 m) span.

4 Chalk a final mark 6 feet, 8 inches (2 m) beyond the 16th marker.

5 That final mark, 166 feet, 8 inches (50.8 m) from the pin, is how far away a hydrogen electron would be from its nucleus to scale.

HEY, WHAT'S GOING ON?

There's a whole world of its own inside an atom. Of course, in real life all of this would be far too small for us to see. The distance to the hydrogen shell (with its single electron) would be 50,000 times the radius (distance from the center to the edge) of the nucleus. We've had to imagine a little here, but there are about 25 "pinhead radii" to an inch. So 2,000 inches would represent 50,000 times the distance of the radii. And 2,000 inches is the same as 166 feet, 8 inches (50.8 m).

ATOMIC NUMBER: 2	ELECTRONS IN OUTERMOST SHELL: 2
ATOMIC WEIGHT: 4.0026	MELTING POINT: -458°F (-272.2°C)
ELEMENT SYMBOL: He	BOILING POINT: -452.07 °F (-268.93°C)

CHAPTER 2

HELIUM

1 H																	2 He
3 Li	4 Be											5 B	6 C	7 N	8 O	9 F	10 Ne
11 Na	12 Mg											13 Al	14 Si	15 P	16 S	17 Cl	18 Ar
19 K	20 Ca	21 Sc	22 Ti	23 V	24 Cr	25 Mn	26 Fe	27 Co	28 Ni	29 Cu	30 Zn	31 Ga	32 Ge	33 As	34 Se	35 Br	36 Kr
37 Rb	38 Sr	39 Y	40 Zr	41 Nb	42 Mo	43 Tc	44 Ru	45 Rh	46 Pd	47 Ag	48 Cd	49 In	50 Sn	51 Sb	52 Te	53 I	54 Xe
55 Cs	56 Ba		72 Hf	73 Ta	74 W	75 Re	76 Os	77 Ir	78 Pt	79 Au	80 Hg	81 Tl	82 Pb	83 Bi	84 Po	85 At	86 Rn
87 Fr	88 Ra		104 Rf	105 Db	106 Sg	107 Bh	108 Hs	109 Mt	110 Ds	111 Rg	112 Cn	113 Nh	114 Fl	115 Mc	116 Lv	117 Ts	118 Og

57 La	58 Ce	59 Pr	60 Nd	61 Pm	62 Sm	63 Eu	64 Gd	65 Tb	66 Dy	67 Ho	68 Er	69 Tm	70 Yb	71 Lu
89 Ac	90 Th	91 Pa	92 U	93 Np	94 Pu	95 Am	96 Cm	97 Bk	98 Cf	99 Es	100 Fm	101 Md	102 No	103 Lr

Ladies and gentlemen, prepare yourselves for the presence of royalty. You are about to encounter helium, the first of the noble gases. Starting with helium and working down the same column of the periodic table, you find a group of elements that don't mix with others—a bit like the nobility, in fact. And the reason for that snooty attitude can be traced to electrons. Each of the noble gas elements has a full set of electrons in its outer shell: two for helium and eight for all the others. That means that they're not on the lookout for other elements to link up with in order to gain or lose electrons. Or, to put it more chemically, helium and the other noble gases are unlikely to *react* with anything else.

WHAT DOES HELIUM LOOK LIKE?

Helium, like the other elements in its column, is colorless and odorless. Take a look at the temperatures for helium. There's only a few degrees of difference between its melting point and its boiling point. What's more, go about a degree colder than its melting point, and you reach absolute zero, or −459.7°F (−273.15°C). It's the lowest possible temperature, where nothing could be colder.

What does all that mean? Well, it means that helium is almost always in the form of a gas—a noble gas, in fact. And you'll find a similar story for all the noble gases in helium's column. They may not melt at quite as low a temperature as helium, but they remain liquid for only a few degrees before becoming invisible gases.

WHEN WAS HELIUM DISCOVERED?

By the 1800s, scientists had developed a way of detecting substances even in the most distant stars. They would pass the light from those sources through a prism, which would break it up into its component colors. It's a bit like looking at a rainbow. Elements would leave a pattern of lines and color bands across the light spectrum—that pattern was the element's "fingerprint."

Jules Janssen

In 1868, French astronomer Jules Janssen passed sunlight through a prism during a solar eclipse (when the Moon passes in front of the Sun). He detected a yellow line that seemed, at first, to be a sign of the element sulfur. Two British scientists, Norman Lockyer and Edward Frankland, noticed the same yellow line, but they concluded that it was a new element (not sulfur). Over the next few years, more and more scientists came to agree with the British pair, and it was Lockyer's name for the new element that stuck—helium, from the Greek word for the Sun, *helios*.

SPECTRUM

The broad range of visible light (colors ranging from red to violet) and other forms of radiation (such as gamma rays or infrared rays) that is absorbed or sent out by an object. Each element affects how we see the spectrum of light coming from an object.

WHERE IS HELIUM USED?

Many people laugh when they first come across helium—not a claim that many elements can make! That's because it is the gas inside floating party balloons. You might have seen people inhaling some of that gas and then talking: For a few seconds they sound like Donald Duck or SpongeBob. That's because the helium causes the person's vocal cords to vibrate at a faster rate. It's not wise to inhale gases, but those funny voices, and the fact that helium balloons float up to the ceiling or the sky, indicate that helium is lighter than air.

The lightness of helium makes it useful (but a bit expensive) for inflating larger balloons and even airships, and the fact that it doesn't react with other elements is another big advantage. Helium is used to force rocket fuel out of its tank. Liquid helium is so extremely cold that it is helpful in cooling the magnets in modern medical equipment, like giant MRI scanners.

An isotope of helium, known as Helium-3, might become a safe and pollution-free fuel in the future. It's rare on Earth, but scientists believe that it is plentiful on the Moon . . . which might be a reason to set up a Moon base one day.

ISOTOPE

A version of an element that has more or fewer neutrons than it has protons.

THE BIG BANG

Most scientists now believe that the universe began in a huge explosion (called the Big Bang) about 14 billion years ago. Before that explosion, the entire universe was inside an unbelievably hot, dense — and tiny — bubble. Then it blew up and expanded, creating time, space, and matter. In a split second it was larger than a galaxy, and it has continued to grow at an amazing rate.

In less than a second after the Big Bang, as the universe began to expand and cool, energy turned into particles of matter and antimatter. Most of these particles destroyed one another because they are opposites, but some matter remained as positively charged protons and neutrally charged neutrons. Over the next three minutes, the universe cooled enough for these to become hydrogen (one proton) and helium (two protons) nuclei. It took another 300,000 years for these nuclei to grab negatively charged electrons to become hydrogen and helium atoms.

ANTIMATTER

All of the elements have "mirror image" counterparts, consisting of antiparticles, which have the same weight as normal electrons and protons but an opposite charge from the familiar particles. An enormous amount of energy is released when matter and antimatter touch and cancel each other out.

Meet the Relatives

THE ARISTOCRATS OF THE PERIODIC TABLE

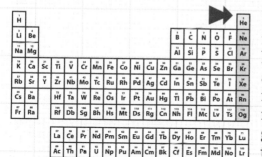

Echoing the behavior of human nobles, like dukes, counts, and barons, helium is part of an elite minority of noble gases, with few relatives. The "unlikely to react" quality of these elements can be turned to advantage. Xenon (Xe), for example, is often used in general anesthesia (the gas that puts you to sleep during surgery). Even a small amount of xenon can reduce uncomfortable side effects from anesthesia, because xenon's stable electrons won't interact with the body's cells.

DANGER LEVEL

☢ ☢ ☢ ☢ ☢

Helium is not toxic in itself, but people should not inhale helium so they can talk in that funny voice. Why should that be, if helium is not toxic? Well, if you inhale helium, it means you're not inhaling air . . . which includes the oxygen that we all need to live. And going without oxygen for too long is definitely dangerous!

EXPERIMENT with the ELEMENT

Being a stable noble element, helium is a safe gas for experiments. The following experiment investigates why helium balloons float, but also how those same balloons would behave if the temperature changed.

HEY, COOL IT!

We've all seen how helium balloons float—and how they float away into the sky if you let go of the string. The floating bit can be explained pretty easily: Helium is a light element and is less dense (fewer molecules in the same volume) than the air around it. But would that still be true if the helium were cooled?

Let's see what happens. Oh—and be sure to do this experiment *inside*. The balloons are meant to hit the ceiling and stop there!

YOU WILL NEED

- ◆ **2 balloons (roughly the same size) filled with helium (available at party stores and some large supermarkets)**
- ◆ **Friend to help**
- ◆ **Watch with second hand or timer**
- ◆ **Paper and pencil**
- ◆ **Freezer large enough to hold one of the balloons**

1. Hold the first balloon right down at the floor and ask a friend to prepare to record a time.

2. At a given signal, let go of the balloon and have your friend time how many seconds it takes to hit the ceiling. Write down your results.

3. Do the same for the second balloon.

4 Now put the second balloon in the freezer.

5 After 30 minutes, remove the balloon from the freezer.

6 Hold the balloons side by side and notice any differences.

7 Time how long each balloon takes to rise, releasing the second (freezer) balloon first. Note any differences in times.

8 Finally, wait another 15 minutes and time the two balloons once more.

HEY, WHAT'S GOING ON?

Cooling the gas in the freezer means that the helium molecules move around less and take up less space, so the helium becomes denser. Remember, helium balloons rise because the helium in them is less dense than the air around them. But now the colder helium becomes less likely to float because the density is closer to that of the outside air.

ATOMIC NUMBER: 5	ELECTRONS IN OUTERMOST SHELL: 3
ATOMIC WEIGHT: 10.8111	MELTING POINT: 3,769°F (2,076°C)
ELEMENT SYMBOL: B	BOILING POINT: 7,101°F (3,927°C)

CHAPTER 3

BORON

1 H																	2 He
3 Li	4 Be											5 B	6 C	7 N	8 O	9 F	10 Ne
11 Na	12 Mg											13 Al	14 Si	15 P	16 S	17 Cl	18 Ar
19 K	20 Ca	21 Sc	22 Ti	23 V	24 Cr	25 Mn	26 Fe	27 Co	28 Ni	29 Cu	30 Zn	31 Ga	32 Ge	33 As	34 Se	35 Br	36 Kr
37 Rb	38 Sr	39 Y	40 Zr	41 Nb	42 Mo	43 Tc	44 Ru	45 Rh	46 Pd	47 Ag	48 Cd	49 In	50 Sn	51 Sb	52 Te	53 I	54 Xe
55 Cs	56 Ba		72 Hf	73 Ta	74 W	75 Re	76 Os	77 Ir	78 Pt	79 Au	80 Hg	81 Tl	82 Pb	83 Bi	84 Po	85 At	86 Rn
87 Fr	88 Ra		104 Rf	105 Db	106 Sg	107 Bh	108 Hs	109 Mt	110 Ds	111 Rg	112 Cn	113 Nh	114 Fl	115 Mc	116 Lv	117 Ts	118 Og

57 La	58 Ce	59 Pr	60 Nd	61 Pm	62 Sm	63 Eu	64 Gd	65 Tb	66 Dy	67 Ho	68 Er	69 Tm	70 Yb	71 Lu
89 Ac	90 Th	91 Pa	92 U	93 Np	94 Pu	95 Am	96 Cm	97 Bk	98 Cf	99 Es	100 Fm	101 Md	102 No	103 Lr

You'd have thought that with a seemingly boring name like boron, this element might be a loner, with no contact with other elements in the form of compounds (see page 22). In fact, boron atoms form strong attachments with atoms from many of those other elements. Boron has been used for thousands of years in the form of one of those compounds (borax), and it's useful in helping other elements team up and do all kinds of cool stuff. That behind-the-scenes quality makes boron one of the most useful of all the elements.

WHAT DOES BORON LOOK LIKE?

Good question. Very few people have seen pure boron because it's so uncommon on its own in nature. That's because it links up with other elements to form secure compounds, usually held together with covalent bonds. The most familiar of those compounds is known as borax, which is boron mixed with atoms of sodium, oxygen, and hydrogen. Borax is a white powder that has long been used to boost laundry detergent.

COMPOUND

A compound is a chemical made from the atoms of different elements and held together by chemical bonds. Those bonds involve swapping or sharing electrons so that the different atoms can have a stable outer shell of electrons (remember—eight electrons in a stable outer shell). An ionic bond is formed by swapping electrons between the atoms. A covalent bond involves atoms sharing electrons.

WHEN WAS BORON DISCOVERED?

People had been noticing and using boron for hundreds —maybe thousands—of years before anyone knew it was a separate element. Its name even comes from the word that ancient Arabs gave to the powdery compound borax (*burqa*). Trade routes between Asia (where borax was first mined) and Europe brought it to people's attention during the Middle Ages.

SIR HUMPHRY DAVY

Eighteenth-century scientists had produced a weak acid—known as boric acid— by adding minerals to borax. A century later, Englishman Sir Humphry Davy and other scientists tried and failed to isolate boron from that acid. They knew it was there, but it was only in 1909 that Ezekiel Weintraub of the General Electric Company produced boron in its pure form.

WHERE IS BORON USED?

Talk about an unsung hero. For a nondescript powder that took people centuries to isolate as an element in its own right, boron seems to crop up all over the place. It still has a big role in laundry and cleaning products, but about 70 percent of the boron in the United States is used to produce glass and ceramics. It's also a useful insecticide and an ingredient in semiconductors, magnets, and other high-tech products, and it makes a compound (when combined with nitrogen) that's almost as hard as diamonds. Boron is also essential for the safe running of nuclear reactors because it captures neutrons released as nuclear reactions take place. A buildup of neutrons

would otherwise lead to an uncontrolled nuclear reaction—not good.

Many of the images of the 16th-century Queen Elizabeth I of England show her as having very white skin. Artists and royal poets praised the Queen's "beautiful fair complexion" (don't forget, her father, King Henry VIII, had a nasty habit of beheading people who displeased him). It now seems certain that the whiteness came from borax powder, which the queen used on her face even into old age. Borax powder can irritate the skin, especially over long periods. And since Elizabeth took a bath only once a month—jealous?—things probably got pretty itchy for her.

Meet the Relatives

GROUP 13: METALS, OR WHAT?

1 H																	2 He
3 Li	4 Be											5 B	6 C	7 N	8 O	9 F	10 Ne
11 Na	12 Mg											13 Al	14 Si	15 P	16 S	17 Cl	18 Ar
19 K	20 Ca	21 Sc	22 Ti	23 V	24 Cr	25 Mn	26 Fe	27 Co	28 Ni	29 Cu	30 Zn	31 Ga	32 Ge	33 As	34 Se	35 Br	36 Kr
37 Rb	38 Sr	39 Y	40 Zr	41 Nb	42 Mo	43 Tc	44 Ru	45 Rh	46 Pd	47 Ag	48 Cd	49 In	50 Sn	51 Sb	52 Te	53 I	54 Xe
55 Cs	56 Ba		72 Hf	73 Ta	74 W	75 Re	76 Os	77 Ir	78 Pt	79 Au	80 Hg	81 Tl	82 Pb	83 Bi	84 Po	85 At	86 Rn
87 Fr	88 Ra		104 Rf	105 Db	106 Sg	107 Bh	108 Hs	109 Mt	110 Ds	111 Rg	112 Cn	113 Nh	114 Fl	115 Mc	116 Lv	117 Ts	118 Og

57 La	58 Ce	59 Pr	60 Nd	61 Pm	62 Sm	63 Eu	64 Gd	65 Tb	66 Dy	67 Ho	68 Er	69 Tm	70 Yb	71 Lu
89 Ac	90 Th	91 Pa	92 U	93 Np	94 Pu	95 Am	96 Cm	97 Bk	98 Cf	99 Es	100 Fm	101 Md	102 No	103 Lr

Usually all the elements in a column (group) of the periodic table have pretty similar properties—even if some of the ones lower down are "super" versions of the ones higher up. So when you look down helium's column, for example, you'll see elements that we know mainly as gases that don't react with other elements.

Many of the other groups have the word "metal" in their name—in fact, most elements are one type of metal or another. And what makes

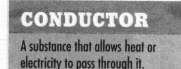
something a metal? Well, most metals are strong and dense, solid at room temperature, and good conductors of heat and electricity, and they make a "ping" when you hit them (think of metal bells). Nonmetals are pretty much the opposite in most of these categories—low-density and weak, maybe or maybe not solid at room temperature, poor conductors, and more likely to make a "thud" if you hit them (imagine ringing a bell made of bones, which consist of the nonmetallic element calcium).

That's clear enough—elements are one thing or the other. But wait! Boron is considered to be a metalloid, with some properties of a metal (it is hard) and some of nonmetals (it doesn't conduct heat or electricity well). But if you look down boron's column on the periodic table, the elements become more and more like metals the farther down you go.

DANGER LEVEL

Boron is not really dangerous, and our bodies do need some boron for healthy bones. Normally any excess boron that we consume in bananas, raisins, and other food can be passed in urine.

EXPERIMENT *with the* **ELEMENT**

Many elements form crystals. A crystal develops when the element's molecules are arranged in a repeating pattern. Crystals are solids with flat sides and symmetrical shapes. Boron forms crystals readily, as you'll see in the following experiment. You can check the different crystal shapes that are produced, all growing from a familiar shape—a star!

A STAR IS BORON

The element boron forms crystals pretty naturally, and in this experiment you can help that process along. And because other elements you'll read about here are also crystals— or sometimes form them—you'll have something extremely cool to remember as you learn about their properties.

It's too bad that it's not so easy to make the crystal form of the next element, carbon (see page 31). You've probably heard of those crystals—they're called diamonds!

YOU WILL NEED

- ◆ **Pipe cleaners**
- ◆ **Widemouthed jar (1 pint or 500 ml)**
- ◆ **String**
- ◆ **Scissors**
- ◆ **Pencil**
- ◆ **Boiling water**
- ◆ **Spoon**
- ◆ **Borax (available as 20 Mule Team Borax Laundry Booster in laundry section of grocery stores)**

WARNING! Get an adult to pour the boiling water and to handle the borax.

1 Shape the pipe cleaner into a star shape, with the ends meeting to form the fifth pointed side. Make sure the star will fit inside the jar.

2 Tie one end of the string to one of the points of the star-shaped pipe cleaner.

3 Use the scissors to cut the string long enough for the "star" to hang midway down the jar from its mouth.

4 Tie the other end of the string to the pencil.

5 Have an adult pour boiling water into the jar, almost to the top.

6 Add a spoonful of borax to the water and stir until it's dissolved.

7 Repeat Step 6 until it's impossible to dissolve all of the borax.

8 Hang the star so the pencil rests on the lid of the jar and the star is suspended in the liquid, not touching the bottom.

9 Leave overnight, preferably in a relatively warm spot (like near a radiator).

10 The next morning, pull out your crystal. You're a star!

HEY, WHAT'S GOING ON?

Borax is a compound of boron and several other elements, but like boron itself, it forms a crystal structure. This chemistry experiment, like the cooled helium balloon (see page 16), shows the effect of temperature on reactions. Here, the molecules of hot water move farther apart from one another, allowing more of the borax crystals to dissolve. As the water cools and evaporates overnight, there's less room for the borax crystals to stay in the water solution. Crystals begin to form, building on each other as there's less and less water to hold them.

	ATOMIC NUMBER: 6	ELECTRONS IN OUTERMOST SHELL: 4
	ATOMIC WEIGHT: 12.0107	MELTING POINT: 6,381°F (3,527°C)
	ELEMENT SYMBOL: C	BOILING POINT: 7,281°F (4,027°C)

CHAPTER 4

CARBON

Let's face it: Carbon is probably the most important element in the whole periodic table. OK, OK, you'll hear people saying we need oxygen to breathe, or nitrogen to make sure plants grow, or ytterbium to . . . do whatever ytterbium does. But for downright versatility and overall worth (think of diamonds!), it's hard to beat carbon.

It makes up so much of everything in our everyday lives. We need it for charcoal. We write with it. We wear it on our finger when we get engaged. We drive our cars with it. But even beyond that, scientists point out that life as we know it is based on carbon. And by that they mean the rich variety of compounds that carbon makes with other elements—the same compounds that they keep hoping to find elsewhere in the universe to determine whether there's alien life out there.

WHAT DOES CARBON LOOK LIKE?

Black. And solid. Wait—that's not much of an answer for what's considered to be the most vital element of the periodic table, at least for us humans and other life-forms. But carbon, in its purest form and at the temperatures we're comfortable with, really does look black. Even its name comes from the Latin word *carbo*, meaning "charcoal." (Yes, we really do barbecue our hamburgers and hot dogs with lumps of the element carbon.) But bond those carbon atoms together differently, and you get graphite (the stuff at the tip of your pencil). Both of those versions of carbon are pretty soft. Try a different pattern of bonded atoms, and you get something harder, like coal, or even diamonds.

Those things are all just pure carbon. Now see what happens when you get it bonding with other elements. It's what makes us tick, powers our cars, sweetens our food . . . and might destroy the world with the greenhouse effect. That's the term for how excess carbon dioxide in the Earth's atmosphere acts like a blanket and prevents heat from escaping—just as a greenhouse keeps heat inside its glass walls.

WHEN WAS CARBON DISCOVERED?

Well, even before the Romans came up with the word *carbo*, the Greeks had named another form of carbon—graphite. They knew it as *grapho*, meaning "to draw or write." And the Chinese had been familiar with diamonds since 2500 BCE, using them to make strong tools as well as beautiful jewelry. But it was during the great period of the Scientific Revolution in the 18th century that observers really came to understand carbon as an element.

Scientists by that time knew that after charcoal was burned in a closed container, the remaining ash weighed less than the original charcoal. The missing mass must have gone somewhere—but where? (We now know that the carbon had combined with the oxygen in the air to produce the compound carbon dioxide.) In 1772, French scientist Antoine Lavoisier put a diamond in a closed glass jar and used a magnifying glass to burn it—talk about an expensive experiment. He measured the amount of carbon dioxide and saw that it matched

WAITING THOUSANDS OF YEARS FOR A DATE?

Like all elements, carbon has a fixed number of protons in its nucleus—the atomic number. But the number of neutrons can vary. These different versions (with different numbers of neutrons) are called isotopes of that element. One carbon isotope, carbon-14, has eight neutrons. Add these to the six protons (carbon's atomic number), and you get 14.

Carbon-14 is in the air, and all living things absorb it. But when the organism dies, the amount of carbon-14 present in the dead organism decays at a steady rate. Scientists can work out how old a dead organism is by measuring the carbon-14 in it: They know how fast the carbon-14 decays, so they can work back to find out how many years it took from the time the organism died (and stopped absorbing the carbon-14).

Archaeologists have used this "carbon dating" to work out the ages of all kinds of organic matter, such as Egyptian artifacts, the Dead Sea Scrolls, the frozen body of a hunter who died in the European Alps more than 6,000 years ago, and Japanese plant fossils that are over 50,000 years old.

the amount produced by the same amount of charcoal, proving that diamonds were just another form of carbon. Seventeen years later, Lavoisier gave the element its official name.

The link between the different forms of carbon—especially coal, charcoal, graphite, and diamonds—has intrigued people for years. One of Superman's coolest tricks—in addition to the powers of flight, X-ray vision, and super speed—is squeezing a piece of coal *really* hard until it becomes a diamond. Far-fetched? Well, in 1955, scientists at the General Electric Company showed that with enough heat and pressure, graphite could be transformed into diamonds.

WHERE IS CARBON USED?

Carbon's atoms can bond together on their own (ranging from graphite to diamonds) or with the atoms of other elements, making carbon about the most wide-ranging of all elements. Pure carbon is versatile. Its softest version (graphite) is used for writing and as a lubricant. Coal and charcoal are still important fuel sources, and diamonds remain the hardest natural substances on the planet.

Of course you know that diamonds make stunning and expensive jewelry. But did you also know that they have another important quality that helps in industry? They conduct heat better than nearly any other material. That means that when their hardness is put to use (say, as drill bits), diamonds are able to get rid of the heat created by the intense friction of metals grinding together.

But it's in combination with other elements that carbon shows its real versatility. There's even an entire branch of chemistry—organic chemistry—that concentrates on matter that contains carbon. For example, carbon teamed up with hydrogen creates many compounds. One of those, methane (see sidebar, page 35), is the main component of natural gas.

Carbon can form far more complicated bonds, often with a combination of elements, to produce compounds that are used in just about every industry. Hydrocarbons (another carbon–hydrogen compound) are vital fuel sources. Plastics also depend on carbon, and steel gets its strength from carbon combined with iron.

A SIMPLE COMPOUND?

Methane, a compound of carbon and hydrogen, is an excellent example of a covalent bond and the "octet rule" in action. Carbon has four valence (outer shell) electrons, but it needs another four to have its magic number of eight electrons in the outer shell. Hydrogen has just one electron, but the first electron shell fills with two—not eight—electrons. So each hydrogen atom needs another electron so that *its* shell can become stable.

The solution? Team up and share. Four hydrogen atoms bond with one carbon atom and share the total number of outer-shell electrons. Carbon gets to share the four electrons that hydrogen brings to the mix (giving it eight). Meanwhile, each hydrogen atom shares one of the four original carbon electrons (so that each hydrogen atom gets a full pair of electrons).

You can work out this mix by looking at methane's chemical formula: CH_4. That's just another way of saying that each methane molecule contains one carbon atom and four hydrogen atoms.

GERMANIUM: A HUNCH PAYS OFF

1 H																	2 He
3 Li	4 Be											5 B	6 C	7 N	8 O	9 F	10 Ne
11 Na	12 Mg											13 Al	14 Si	15 P	16 S	17 Cl	18 Ar
19 K	20 Ca	21 Sc	22 Ti	23 V	24 Cr	25 Mn	26 Fe	27 Co	28 Ni	29 Cu	30 Zn	31 Ga	32 Ge	33 As	34 Se	35 Br	36 Kr
37 Rb	38 Sr	39 Y	40 Zr	41 Nb	42 Mo	43 Tc	44 Ru	45 Rh	46 Pd	47 Ag	48 Cd	49 In	50 Sn	51 Sb	52 Te	53 I	54 Xe
55 Cs	56 Ba		72 Hf	73 Ta	74 W	75 Re	76 Os	77 Ir	78 Pt	79 Au	80 Hg	81 Tl	82 Pb	83 Bi	84 Po	85 At	86 Rn
87 Fr	88 Ra		104 Rf	105 Db	106 Sg	107 Bh	108 Hs	109 Mt	110 Ds	111 Rg	112 Cn	113 Nh	114 Fl	115 Mc	116 Lv	117 Ts	118 Og

57 La	58 Ce	59 Pr	60 Nd	61 Pm	62 Sm	63 Eu	64 Gd	65 Tb	66 Dy	67 Ho	68 Er	69 Tm	70 Yb	71 Lu
89 Ac	90 Th	91 Pa	92 U	93 Np	94 Pu	95 Am	96 Cm	97 Bk	98 Cf	99 Es	100 Fm	101 Md	102 No	103 Lr

Look closely at the periodic table and count the columns from left to right. You'll see that carbon is in column 14. Now it's time to use a little imagination. Try to imagine the table without that funny bit in the middle—columns 3 through 12. That middle bit contains what are called the transition metals, and some of the neat "look down the column to see the same behavior" rules don't work as normal. Now jump from column 2 to column 14 and think of column 14 as "4" instead. That makes things easier, because each column number matches the number of valence (outer shell) electrons the elements in that column have.

Dmitri Mendeleev

That's the sort of thinking that led Dmitri Mendeleev to leave blanks when he compiled the first version of a periodic table of elements in 1869. Silicon (Si) was directly beneath carbon (as it still is in modern tables), and he knew that tin (Sn) also belonged in that column because of its behavior. But he knew that tin couldn't come directly under silicon because of its mass, so Mendeleev left a blank—and let others go and find the missing element.

That happened in 1886, when Clemens A. Winkler discovered just such an element and named it after his native country, Germany—the element we know as germanium (Ge).

DANGER LEVEL

On its own, carbon is not really harmful, but since it lies at the heart of so many compounds, you've got to be careful with it. One of the most deadly—and most basic—of those compounds is a simple carbon-oxygen compound known as carbon monoxide (CO), or the nasty stuff emitted from a car's exhaust pipe. Breathing in carbon monoxide reduces the blood's ability to carry oxygen, which could lead to death.

EXPERIMENT *with the* ELEMENT

Carbon atoms can bond together in several forms, called allotropes (see page 136). Charcoal, graphite, and diamond all look and feel different, but they are simply allotropes of carbon. And the differences go beyond just how they look and feel. Diamond, for example, doesn't conduct electricity, but graphite does—even just a single mark of graphite, as you'll see in the following experiment.

GOOD CONDUCT AWARD

This neat experiment will demonstrate how graphite—even a line of graphite on a sheet of paper—will conduct electricity. It's simple and quick, but it can also prompt you to think of some questions about what is called resistance—the opposite of conductivity—in electricity. For example, does the light shine as brightly if you run the clip up and down the graphite line? If not, why not?

YOU WILL NEED

- ◆ **2 alligator clips with wires attached**
- ◆ **9V battery**
- ◆ **Small LED bulb (with both wires exposed)**
- ◆ **Graphite pencil**
- ◆ **Sheet of construction paper**
- ◆ **Electrical tape**

METHOD

1 Clip one wire to the positive terminal of the battery.

2 Clip the other end of that wire to one LED wire.

3 Clip the second wire to the negative terminal of the battery.

4 Use the pencil to make a thick mark about 4 inches long and 1 inch wide on the paper.

5 Tape the second LED wire to the paper, making sure it's touching the graphite line.

6 Touch the clip from the negative terminal to the graphite line.

7 The LED should light up.

HEY, WHAT'S GOING ON?

Electrons move along the flat planes of the graphite as if they were moving along a wire. The flow is enough to power the LED bulb. You've used the conductivity of the graphite to create an electrical circuit. Here's how it works: Electrons passed from the battery through the wire to the LED, powering the light. The electrons continue along this circuit from the LED wire and through the graphite. Touching the second clip to the graphite completes the circuit by allowing the electrons to pass back to the battery. That's the power of the pencil in action.

But don't forget that the experiment won't work with every carbon allotrope, so don't bother trying it with a string of priceless diamonds!

ATOMIC NUMBER: 7	ELECTRONS IN OUTERMOST SHELL: 5
ATOMIC WEIGHT: 14.0067	MELTING POINT: -346°F (-210°C)
ELEMENT SYMBOL: N	BOILING POINT: -320.43°F (-195.79°C)

CHAPTER 5
NITROGEN

1 H																	2 He
3 Li	4 Be											5 B	6 C	7 N	8 O	9 F	10 Ne
11 Na	12 Mg											13 Al	14 Si	15 P	16 S	17 Cl	18 Ar
19 K	20 Ca	21 Sc	22 Ti	23 V	24 Cr	25 Mn	26 Fe	27 Co	28 Ni	29 Cu	30 Zn	31 Ga	32 Ge	33 As	34 Se	35 Br	36 Kr
37 Rb	38 Sr	39 Y	40 Zr	41 Nb	42 Mo	43 Tc	44 Ru	45 Rh	46 Pd	47 Ag	48 Cd	49 In	50 Sn	51 Sb	52 Te	53 I	54 Xe
55 Cs	56 Ba		72 Hf	73 Ta	74 W	75 Re	76 Os	77 Ir	78 Pt	79 Au	80 Hg	81 Tl	82 Pb	83 Bi	84 Po	85 At	86 Rn
87 Fr	88 Ra		104 Rf	105 Db	106 Sg	107 Bh	108 Hs	109 Mt	110 Ds	111 Rg	112 Cn	113 Nh	114 Fl	115 Mc	116 Lv	117 Ts	118 Og

57 La	58 Ce	59 Pr	60 Nd	61 Pm	62 Sm	63 Eu	64 Gd	65 Tb	66 Dy	67 Ho	68 Er	69 Tm	70 Yb	71 Lu
89 Ac	90 Th	91 Pa	92 U	93 Np	94 Pu	95 Am	96 Cm	97 Bk	98 Cf	99 Es	100 Fm	101 Md	102 No	103 Lr

You know you're important when there's a whole group named after you. Think of all those "oldies" vinyl records, CDs, or MP3s in your parents' (or grandparents') collection—Diana Ross and the Supremes, Buddy Holly and the Crickets, Prince and the Revolution. Now you can add another name to that list: Nitrogen and the Pnictogen Elements. OK, maybe it's not quite in the same category, but nitrogen really does have a group named after it. Column 15 of the periodic table is called the nitrogen family, or the pnictogens. And once you realize how powerful and important nitrogen is—it makes up nearly 80 percent of our atmosphere, for starters—you'll understand why.

WHAT DOES NITROGEN LOOK LIKE?

Unless you turn the thermostat *way* down to about -350°F, you'll only come across nitrogen as a colorless, odorless gas. And there's lots of it—mainly above you and in the air you breathe. Most of that nitrogen is in the form of a molecule of two nitrogen atoms (N_2) that makes up 78 percent of the Earth's atmosphere. Most of those molecules were blown out from volcanoes early in the Earth's history, billions of years ago. By comparison, nitrogen makes up only 0.002 percent of the Earth's crust.

WHEN WAS NITROGEN DISCOVERED?

During the Scientific Revolution in the mid- to late 1700s, when Europeans were coming up with all sorts of discoveries and observations, scientists were intrigued by what had always seemed to be an element in its own right—air. By the 1770s, it was clear that air contained at least two elements, both of them gases. One of those gases allowed things to burn. (It would soon be called oxygen.) The other gas didn't. We now know the other is carbon dioxide, although back then it was usually called "fixed air."

In 1772, Scottish scientist Daniel Rutherford began examining "fixed air." Following earlier experiments, he burned a candle in a closed chamber. The flame went out, so he now had a chamber full of the fixed air. But that wasn't enough. Rutherford then passed that air through lime (a calcium-based powder), which he knew would absorb this fixed air. But he was still left with a third gas—that's when he knew he had found a new element. He called it "noxious air," meaning poisonous air, but the element was officially named nitrogen in 1790.

WHERE IS NITROGEN USED?

The N_2 version of nitrogen that's so widespread in the atmosphere hardly reacts with anything else. Those triple bonds (see page 45) are so strong that the electrons—the heart of any chemical reaction—stay locked into the molecules. That can be a big help, though. Nitrogen gas is used to preserve foods such as fresh vegetables, pasta, and frozen pizza (protecting them from oxygen, which sets off the process of rotting, for example). And scientists use liquid nitrogen when performing low-temperature experiments and to preserve blood and other biological samples.

Those applications all benefit from the "doesn't like to react" feature of N_2. On its own, though, things are different. Nitrogen could almost beat carbon one-on-one in a Most Essential to Life World Championship. This is the plain old N version—the one that *does* react with other elements. In fact, it often links up incredibly strongly with other elements using the same triple-bond arrangement that it uses to bond with itself.

For instance, N is an essential part of DNA, the molecule that has the code for the growth and development of all living organisms—not too shabby! Plants depend on nitrogen, but most of them can't get it directly from the air when it's in its pure form. Instead, plants absorb it from compounds in the ground containing nitrogen. That means that one of the most common uses of nitrogen is in producing the fertilizer ammonia (NH_3) to make plants grow strong and in larger numbers.

TRIPLE BONDS

One of the strongest bonds in all of chemistry involves nitrogen—teaming up with itself! It's not the only element whose atoms achieve a "full set" of outer-shell electrons by finding another of their own. Hydrogen and oxygen also form diatomic (two-atom) molecules—H_2 and O_2—as do four other elements.

Do a little quick arithmetic. If two nitrogen atoms get together, how many pairs do they need to share to reach that magic number of eight? Well, since the first nitrogen atom already has five electrons out there, then it needs to bond with three from the other to reach eight (the octet). And the other nitrogen atom also needs three more, but luckily three of its electrons have already bonded with three from the first nitrogen atom. The result is that three pairs of electrons are shared—in a triple bond, so that each nitrogen atom gets its octet. Remember that each pairing strengthens the bond amazingly. Nitrogen, with its triple bond, is incredibly strong and hardly reacts with anything else, because it doesn't need to!

Meet the Relatives

CYCLES OF LIFE

1 H																	2 He
3 Li	4 Be											5 B	6 C	7 N	8 O	9 F	10 Ne
11 Na	12 Mg											13 Al	14 Si	15 P	16 S	17 Cl	18 Ar
19 K	20 Ca	21 Sc	22 Ti	23 V	24 Cr	25 Mn	26 Fe	27 Co	28 Ni	29 Cu	30 Zn	31 Ga	32 Ge	33 As	34 Se	35 Br	36 Kr
37 Rb	38 Sr	39 Y	40 Zr	41 Nb	42 Mo	43 Tc	44 Ru	45 Rh	46 Pd	47 Ag	48 Cd	49 In	50 Sn	51 Sb	52 Te	53 I	54 Xe
55 Cs	56 Ba		72 Hf	73 Ta	74 W	75 Re	76 Os	77 Ir	78 Pt	79 Au	80 Hg	81 Tl	82 Pb	83 Bi	84 Po	85 At	86 Rn
87 Fr	88 Ra		104 Rf	105 Db	106 Sg	107 Bh	108 Hs	109 Mt	110 Ds	111 Rg	112 Cn	113 Nh	114 Fl	115 Mc	116 Lv	117 Ts	118 Og

57 La	58 Ce	59 Pr	60 Nd	61 Pm	62 Sm	63 Eu	64 Gd	65 Tb	66 Dy	67 Ho	68 Er	69 Tm	70 Yb	71 Lu
89 Ac	90 Th	91 Pa	92 U	93 Np	94 Pu	95 Am	96 Cm	97 Bk	98 Cf	99 Es	100 Fm	101 Md	102 No	103 Lr

Phosphorus (P), the explosive element at the tip of a matchstick, is right below nitrogen in group 15 and shares some of nitrogen's importance to human life. And just as scientists speak of a "nitrogen cycle" of plants absorbing nitrogen from the soil and then animals absorbing nitrogen from those plants and depositing it in the soil as waste, the "phosphorus cycle" tracks the movement of phosphorus, another life-sustaining element from soil to plants to animals and back to the soil again. Even the small amounts of phosphorus that organisms absorb from this cycle are vital for cell development.

DANGER LEVEL

*Nitro*glycerin . . . TNT (ri*nitro*toluene) . . . gunpowder (sulfur, carbon, and potassium *nitr*ate) . . . are you beginning to sense that there's more to nitrogen than helping plants grow? Nitrogen plays a part in some of the best-known explosives. But why?

Well, think about how strong those N_2 molecules are. You would need to add a *lot* of energy to pull the two nitrogen atoms apart because of those powerful triple bonds. But what would happen if you did the opposite—got two nitrogen atoms to join together? Well, triple bonds *release* a lot of energy when they're formed! Yes, we're talking explosions here. So although these explosives contain more than just nitrogen to start off with, once they start to react, the nitrogen atoms team up and give the whole thing oomph . . . or a big bang.

EXPERIMENT *with the* ELEMENT

Now you have a chance to figure out how much—if at all—plants really need nitrogen to grow. Time to check on your green thumb.

FIXIN' TO USE SOME NITROGEN

This is a "slow release" experiment to examine how plants benefit from nitrogen that they receive from the soil. In true scientific fashion, you'll be testing a hypothesis—that nitrogen really does help growth. You'll also have a control for comparison—a plant that won't have the nitrogen treatment.

You need to plan ahead for this one—the real action takes place about two weeks after you begin. So ask your Executive Assistant to make sure your calendar is clear!

YOU WILL NEED

- ♦ **6 small plastic flowerpots (roughly 1-cup or 250 mm size)**
- ♦ **Soil for planting**
- ♦ **6 bean seeds**
- ♦ **2 teaspoons (10 ml) of lawn fertilizer**
- ♦ **Water**
- ♦ **Cup measure**
- ♦ **Ruler**
- ♦ **Gloves**

WARNING! Don't handle the fertilizer with your bare hands. The combination of chemicals (featuring nitrogen) helps plants but can also irritate human skin.

METHOD

1 Fill the flowerpots with soil and plant a bean seed in each of them.

2 Wait for the plants to germinate— about two weeks.

3 You're concentrating on two plants for this experiment, so keep them separate (the extra four are backups in case the seeds don't germinate).

4 Add the fertilizer to the cup measure and slowly fill the cup with water, swirling the cup to mix things.

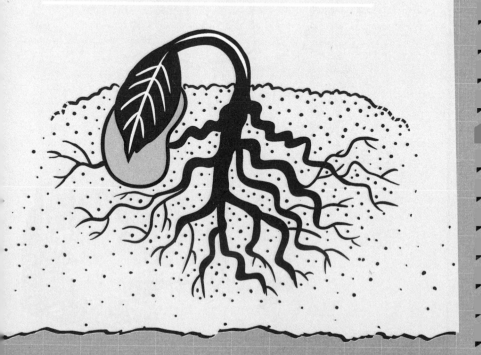

5 Water each plant—one with normal water and the other from the cup you've prepared.

6 Continue watering in this way each day for a week.

7 Use the ruler to measure the plants each morning and check their color.

8 After a week, which plant has grown the most? Does it also look greener?

HEY, WHAT'S GOING ON?

Plants need nitrogen to grow. Although there's lots of nitrogen in the air around us, plants cannot use it. They need to get their nitrogen from the soil, where their roots soak up nutrients. That's why fertilizers containing nitrogen can help plants grow taller and healthier.

That's the heart of the experiment, but you've also done something else very "scientific" here—you've used what's known as the scientific method to make an accurate observation. That means leaving one feature unchanged (in this case, the plant watered with normal water), which is called the "control." You also used at least one "variable" (something that has been changed and compared with the control). The variable in this experiment is the plant watered with the fertilizer mixture. So was your hypothesis correct?

ATOMIC NUMBER: 8		ELECTRONS IN OUTERMOST SHELL: 6
ATOMIC WEIGHT: 15.9994		MELTING POINT: -361.8°F (-218.8°C)
ELEMENT SYMBOL: O		BOILING POINT: -297.4°F (-183°C)

CHAPTER 6
OXYGEN

Take a deep breath in. Now breathe out. You probably knew that the air you just inhaled was a mixture of gases—a mixture of elements, really. Maybe you also knew that of those gases, the most important for us is oxygen. Once air reaches your lungs, it meets millions of tiny cells called alveoli, which absorb oxygen and send it off into the bloodstream. Then it can reach every part of your body, which is definitely important, as well, because your body's metabolism (the way it produces energy from what you eat) depends on oxygen. Just as a fire needs oxygen to burn, your body needs the oxygen in your blood to burn the fuel—sugars and fats—to produce energy.

WHAT DOES OXYGEN LOOK LIKE?

The melting point and boiling point of oxygen are at temperatures so cold it would make even polar bears and penguins shriek. Oxygen only melts at 361.8°F (218.8°C) *below zero*. When things get 63.4°F (−35.8°C) warmer (*that's* warmer?!), it boils and becomes an invisible gas.

That means oxygen here at the Earth's surface, where things tend to be nice and warm, usually shows up as a gas. And that's how we normally encounter it, with every breath we take—even if it's mixed in with other gases. This gas form of oxygen usually comes to us as a molecule of two oxygen atoms, so it's written as O_2. But if somehow you were able to cool your oxygen enough, you'd find that its liquid and solid forms have an amazing light blue color.

WHEN WAS OXYGEN DISCOVERED?

Oxygen, in various compounds, makes up nearly half of the mass of the Earth's crust, two-thirds of the mass of the human body, and nine-tenths of the mass of all the water on our planet—but its identity as a separate element remained hidden until the 18th century.

It was only in 1774 that oxygen was identified as an element. And who did this identifying? That's a toss-up between chemists Carl Wilhelm Scheele of

ANTOINE LAVOISIER

Sweden and Joseph Priestley of England. Each of them had heated up a reddish-colored mineral (now identified as a compound of mercury and oxygen) and produced a gas that caused flames to burn with "amazing strength." That gas, of course, was oxygen. Nowadays, most people credit Priestley, because he published his findings first (even if Scheele probably made his discovery earlier). But the credit for naming oxygen goes to Antoine Lavoisier of France. He named it oxygen (Greek for "acid former") because he thought it was present in all acids. Lavoisier was wrong about the acids, but the name stuck.

WHERE IS OXYGEN USED?

An element that's needed in every breath you take—sounds pretty useful, right? All animals depend on oxygen to help produce energy through a process called respiration. Oxygen makes up about 20 percent of the air around us, so 20 percent of each breath you take is used for respiration. We depend on "standard-issue" oxygen (O_2) for our respiration, and we get rid of the gases we don't need when we breathe out. One of those gases also contains O_2, but combined with the element carbon (C) to produce the molecule carbon dioxide (CO_2).

Plants do the opposite with their respiration—they use CO_2 and get rid of O_2 as they produce energy. And that's why we depend on trees and other plants so much for clean air and a healthy planet. All of these vital stages of respiration depend on a neat feature of oxygen. It's something you've come across many times, even if you didn't know you were making chemical observations. Oxygen can be very greedy, snatching electrons off the surface of most things it touches. Once they've been robbed of those electrons, those other materials change color and often weaken. The process is called oxidation: Want to guess where that word came from?

If you take a bite out of an apple and leave it out for an hour, you come back to find the apple's flesh all brown and discolored. That's because it's been oxidized. Oxygen can also damage metals with a similar "gotcha!" game of tag. Take a look at some rusting iron or tarnished silver: Oxidation strikes again!

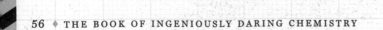

Don't get the idea that oxygen or oxidation are all bad, though. Think of the most important breakthrough for the first human beings: the discovery of fire. What those early humans had actually discovered was a way of controlling oxidation. A fire is simply a special form of

oxidation known as combustion, when the reaction takes place in heat and the fuel (such as wood, coal, or oil) is oxidized. And although fires can be deadly, they can also provide heat to keep us warm and a way to cook up delicious grub.

What's more, combustion is the driving force—literally—of automobiles, which rely on burning fuel to power their "internal combustion" engines. And the rockets that sent NASA astronauts to the Moon used liquid oxygen to power their way out of Earth's orbit. Once again, it was the special powers of oxygen that made all of that possible.

So, from the Stone Age to the Space Age, oxygen has proved to be the element that has kept human beings alive and allowed them to take giant leaps forward. It's just as well that it's the third-most-abundant element in the universe!

Meet the Relatives

SELENIUM: GOING LOCO?

1 H																	2 He
3 Li	4 Be											5 B	6 C	7 N	8 O	9 F	10 Ne
11 Na	12 Mg											13 Al	14 Si	15 P	16 S	17 Cl	18 Ar
19 K	20 Ca	21 Sc	22 Ti	23 V	24 Cr	25 Mn	26 Fe	27 Co	28 Ni	29 Cu	30 Zn	31 Ga	32 Ge	33 As	34 Se	35 Br	36 Kr
37 Rb	38 Sr	39 Y	40 Zr	41 Nb	42 Mo	43 Tc	44 Ru	45 Rh	46 Pd	47 Ag	48 Cd	49 In	50 Sn	51 Sb	52 Te	53 I	54 Xe
55 Cs	56 Ba		72 Hf	73 Ta	74 W	75 Re	76 Os	77 Ir	78 Pt	79 Au	80 Hg	81 Tl	82 Pb	83 Bi	84 Po	85 At	86 Rn
87 Fr	88 Ra		104 Rf	105 Db	106 Sg	107 Bh	108 Hs	109 Mt	110 Ds	111 Rg	112 Cn	113 Nh	114 Fl	115 Mc	116 Lv	117 Ts	118 Og

57 La	58 Ce	59 Pr	60 Nd	61 Pm	62 Sm	63 Eu	64 Gd	65 Tb	66 Dy	67 Ho	68 Er	69 Tm	70 Yb	71 Lu
89 Ac	90 Th	91 Pa	92 U	93 Np	94 Pu	95 Am	96 Cm	97 Bk	98 Cf	99 Es	100 Fm	101 Md	102 No	103 Lr

Just two rows down from oxygen in column 16 is the element selenium (Se). It's in the same group (column) as oxygen, which means that selenium often behaves in a similar way to oxygen when it reacts with other elements. That's because the elements in column 16, often called the chalcogens, have six electrons in their outer shell. They're always on the lookout for two more electrons to fill that layer to make an octet. Oxygen does that by teaming up with two hydrogen atoms (which have one electron each) to form water (H_2O). Selenium does the same thing with hydrogen to form the highly poisonous hydrogen selenide (H_2Se).

Selenium also has some special electrical properties that make it useful. Its resistance to electrical flow depends on the amount of light shining on it. As the light become brighter, the selenium conducts electricity better. That makes it useful in producing light meters and other instruments that need to respond to different light levels. Selenium is also able to produce energy from light, making it a practical component for solar panels.

Selenium is present in the soil, and very small amounts of it are helpful to plants and animals. However, sometimes plants absorb high levels of selenium, making them dangerous for grazing livestock. For example, astragalus, known as "locoweed," looks harmless enough, but eating it can lead to serious damage to the nervous system, and even death. If cows eat too much, they "go loco" by losing control and staggering around in confusion. Cattle ranchers in the Rocky Mountains try to get rid of this wild herb if they see it growing anywhere near their herd.

EXPERIMENT *with the* ELEMENT

Both of the following experiments show the importance of oxygen to the chemical reaction we call combustion. They also shed light on what happens *after* elements combust. The first experiment focuses on carbon dioxide—invisible, yet so different from normal air. The second recalls an experiment first conducted in 1781 by the British scientist Henry Cavendish, who showed that water is another by-product of some combustion.

GLOBAL COOLING

Here's a cool way to learn more about oxygen and how it teams up with one of its periodic table neighbors, carbon. The experiment features burning candles. "Burning" is really another word for combustion, a chemical reaction that depends on oxygen. So if a flame is doused with water or smothered with a blanket, its supply of oxygen is cut off, and the flame goes out.

Those two methods of putting out a flame involve a liquid (the water) or a solid (the blanket). We're going to do the same thing with a gas—and we're going to create that gas in an experiment of our own. Maybe you've done experiments where you mixed baking soda with vinegar or lemon juice to create a rocket or volcano: The rocket blasted off or the volcano erupted because of a gas that your mixture created—carbon dioxide.

Carbon dioxide gets blamed for a lot of global warming. In this experiment, though, it's doing its bit for global *cooling* by extinguishing the flames. It works best—almost like magic—if you do it inside and turn off the lights right after you've mixed the two ingredients.

YOU WILL NEED

- ◆ **8 votive candles**
  (sometimes called tea light candles)
- ◆ **An adult and an assistant**
- ◆ **Matches**
- ◆ **2 tablespoons (30 ml) of baking soda**
- ◆ **Large glass pitcher (2 quarts)**
- ◆ **3 tablespoons (45 ml) of vinegar**
- ◆ **Wooden mixing spoon**

METHOD

1 Line up the candles so they're very close to each other, almost touching, on a table or counter.

2 Ask the adult to light the candles and have your assistant stay close to the room's light switch.

3 Add the baking soda to the pitcher.

Now add the vinegar and mix with the wooden spoon.

 Ask your assistant to turn off the lights. Carefully pick up the pitcher.

6 Hold its spout about 6 inches over the first candle and without letting any liquid out, gently tip the pitcher until the flame goes out.

7 Repeat Step 6 along the line of candles until all eight have been blown out mysteriously.

HEY, WHAT'S GOING ON?

By mixing the vinegar and baking soda, you made two complicated compounds. One of those, known as carbonic acid (H_2CO_3), breaks down into water (H_2O) and carbon dioxide (CO_2). Carbon dioxide is a mixture of one carbon atom with two oxygen atoms. It's invisible, so you can't see it once you've created it in this experiment. But you should also remember that CO_2 is heavier than air, so it sinks through air just as water or juice (also heavier than air) do, so although you can't see it in the pitcher, sure enough it's sitting in there just as water or juice would be. And like water or juice, it can be poured out.

And that's when the fun of this experiment takes over. When you tip the pitcher over the candles one by one, you're actually pouring out the heavy carbon dioxide. It sinks down and displaces the oxygen that's fueling each flame, so the candles go out, one right after the other. Hmmm . . . carbon dioxide usually takes the blame for global warming, but here it's putting out fires!

EXPERIMENT 7 TIME FACTOR: 5 MINUTES

ON THE TRAIL OF CAVENDISH

There's something odd about producing water by burning something. Don't firefighters use giant tanks of water to put out fires? But unexpected things happen when elements get together. Unexpected, that is, unless you have an idea of what to expect. And you will next time, once you've done this experiment. See whether you can gather the same "dew" that chemist Henry Cavendish observed (see page 2) more than 200 years ago.

YOU WILL NEED

- Birthday candle
- Poster tack
- Flat-bottomed plate
- Matches
- Adult to help
- Clear drinking glass

WARNING! MATCH ALERT!

METHOD

1. Poke the base of the candle into a small amount of poster tack.

2. Press the tack into the center of the plate so that the candle is held upright.

3 Have the adult light the candle and let it burn for about 15 seconds.

4 Carefully place the glass upside down on the plate so that it covers the candle.

5 Wait until the candle goes out— it should take a few seconds.

6 Carefully pick up the glass and examine the inside of it.

HEY, WHAT'S GOING ON?

You'll see small drops of liquid on the inside of the glass. These are what Cavendish first described as "dew" before concluding that they were pure water. Like your scientific colleague centuries ago, you just set up a chemical reaction. The candle wax (made of a carbon–hydrogen compound) reacted with the oxygen in the air during the combustion. The result was that versions of those same elements (carbon, hydrogen, and oxygen) were still present, but in different combinations with one another.

Some of the oxygen bonded with the carbon to form carbon dioxide; that gas collected in the glass. The rest of the oxygen combined with the hydrogen in the two-to-one formula that we recognize as water: H_2O. And that's what collected as "dew."

ATOMIC NUMBER: 9	ELECTRONS IN OUTERMOST SHELL: 7
ATOMIC WEIGHT: 18.9984	MELTING POINT: -363.41°F (-219.67°C)
ELEMENT SYMBOL: F	BOILING POINT: -306.6°F (-188.11°C)

CHAPTER 7

FLUORINE

1 H																	2 He
3 Li	4 Be											5 B	6 C	7 N	8 O	9 F	10 Ne
11 Na	12 Mg											13 Al	14 Si	15 P	16 S	17 Cl	18 Ar
19 K	20 Ca	21 Sc	22 Ti	23 V	24 Cr	25 Mn	26 Fe	27 Co	28 Ni	29 Cu	30 Zn	31 Ga	32 Ge	33 As	34 Se	35 Br	36 Kr
37 Rb	38 Sr	39 Y	40 Zr	41 Nb	42 Mo	43 Tc	44 Ru	45 Rh	46 Pd	47 Ag	48 Cd	49 In	50 Sn	51 Sb	52 Te	53 I	54 Xe
55 Cs	56 Ba		72 Hf	73 Ta	74 W	75 Re	76 Os	77 Ir	78 Pt	79 Au	80 Hg	81 Tl	82 Pb	83 Bi	84 Po	85 At	86 Rn
87 Fr	88 Ra		104 Rf	105 Db	106 Sg	107 Bh	108 Hs	109 Mt	110 Ds	111 Rg	112 Cn	113 Nh	114 Fl	115 Mc	116 Lv	117 Ts	118 Og

	57 La	58 Ce	59 Pr	60 Nd	61 Pm	62 Sm	63 Eu	64 Gd	65 Tb	66 Dy	67 Ho	68 Er	69 Tm	70 Yb	71 Lu
	89 Ac	90 Th	91 Pa	92 U	93 Np	94 Pu	95 Am	96 Cm	97 Bk	98 Cf	99 Es	100 Fm	101 Md	102 No	103 Lr

Public health savior or Public Enemy Number One? There aren't many elements that stir up debate the way fluorine does. To be accurate, it's not fluorine itself but some of the compounds it forms that have stirred up this hornet's nest. But considering that they're called "fluorides," it's not surprising that the trail leads directly back to fluorine. By the way, have you noticed where fluorine is on the periodic table? Way over on the right, needing just one more electron to complete its outer shell. That might be a key to what makes it tick: It's crazy about getting "just one more electron, please!" so it reacts at the drop of a hat.

WHAT DOES FLUORINE LOOK LIKE?

If you came across pure fluorine at room temperature—and we don't recommend it!—you'd find a pale yellow gas that is easily flammable. It sits at the top of column 17 of the periodic table with a set of elements known as the halogen group. Like fluorine, they have seven electrons in their outer (valence) shell. That means they need just one more electron to fill it up and become stable.

If fluorine were a human, we'd say it had a desperate need for company. A chemist, though, would probably put it differently, saying something like "fluorine is the most chemically reactive element." Those two descriptions, of course, mean pretty much the same thing, and fluorine reacts with just about every other element except oxygen, helium, neon, and krypton. And those reactions can be pretty intense: If pure fluorine touches almost anything, it will burst into flames.

But those explosions and flames tell us something more about fluorine. Think about it: A big explosion is a sudden release of energy. And that energy was released when fluorine reacted with another element. But after the flame has died away, the fluorine is part of a compound (it's joined to the other element). And if a lot of energy was released to create the compound, then it stands to reason that a lot of energy would have to be *put in* to tear that newly formed compound apart. You don't find that sort of energy too easily in the natural world, which means that fluorine compounds are strong and stable.

WHEN WAS FLUORINE DISCOVERED?

As you might imagine, since fluorine is an element that's always exploding or burning things up in its natural state, we don't ever come across pure fluorine naturally. People came to know fluorine through its compounds, and only then did some very brave scientists recognize it and isolate it. Discovering explosive elements—who said scientists have boring jobs?

GEORGIUS AGRICOLA

We first learned about fluorine through industry. Georgius Agricola, a 16th-century German scientist, was observing how ores were smelted (that's when you apply intense heat and chemicals to separate the pure metals inside). He noted that a mineral called fluorspar (which we now know is a compound of calcium and fluorine) could be added to an ore in the smelting process. Fluorspar has a lower melting point than most ores, so adding it would lower the melting point of the ore, making it easier to extract the metals inside from other compounds.

ORE

Metals are rarely found in their pure form in nature. They are often mixed with other elements, and these mixtures are called ores.

The "fluor" bit of the word fluorspar is a clue. It comes from the Latin word *fluere*, meaning "to flow." So you can see that we were already halfway to isolating fluorine—or at least halfway to getting the word. By the 19th century, scientists were in full swing trying to isolate and identify new elements. But guess what? When they got close to separating fluorine from compounds, they kept getting burned and even blinded.

Still, by 1813, British scientist Sir Humphry Davy had announced the arrival of a new element, which he called fluorine. But he still hadn't produced it in pure form. That had to wait until 1886, when the French chemist Henri Moissan isolated fluorine, after his work had been delayed four times by poisoning.

WHERE IS FLUORINE USED?

The general public mostly knows about the element fluorine because of the compounds it forms with other elements. The most well-known one is fluoride, which we use to fight tooth decay. Many types of toothpaste contain fluoride, and some communities have even chosen to add fluoride to supplies of drinking water as a way of improving people's health. That move has sparked all sorts of controversy (see sidebar).

Fluorides, however, are just the tip of the iceberg. An element as reactive as fluorine is bound to have all sorts of practical uses because it forms so many stable compounds. Those uses range from its role as a rocket fuel (helping the carbon, oxygen, and aluminum to burn) to producing nonstick plastics and substances like Teflon (the smooth cooking surface on frying pans) to microtechnology (allowing technicians to make circuits on microchips). It also combines with chlorine and carbon atoms to produce chlorofluoro-carbons (CFCs), which help refrigerators run. Unfortunately, CFCs also have a terrible effect when they are released, destroying one of the layers of the atmosphere (the ozone layer) that protects us from harmful radiation.

SOMETHING IN THE WATER

Fluorides are compounds that combine fluorine with another element, usually a metal. But the fluorides that you've probably heard of are in toothpaste—and maybe in the water that you drink. Scientists have noted for more than 60 years that fluorides slow the spread of tooth decay. The results were so obvious that the toothpaste industry caught on quickly. So did a number of communities in the United States and in other countries, when they added fluoride to their water supply (we call that "fluoridation").

And that's when the trouble started. Many people opposed the "forced" use of medicine, as they saw it. Others questioned whether fluoride really worked, or even if it was perhaps harmful. Some even said that it could cause cancer because it teamed up with growth cells in the bones, so a cancer would spread quickly.

If you look on the internet, you will find thousands of websites where people make all those accusations. But you'll also find sites that describe fluoridation as a medical triumph that has saved governments billions of dollars in dental expense . . . and helped keep people healthy. That might be one for you to decide.

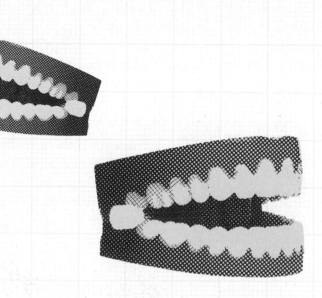

Meet the Relatives 🤝

GROUP 17: WORTH THEIR SALT

1 H																	2 He
3 Li	4 Be											5 B	6 C	7 N	8 O	9 F	10 Ne
11 Na	12 Mg											13 Al	14 Si	15 P	16 S	17 Cl	18 Ar
19 K	20 Ca	21 Sc	22 Ti	23 V	24 Cr	25 Mn	26 Fe	27 Co	28 Ni	29 Cu	30 Zn	31 Ga	32 Ge	33 As	34 Se	35 Br	36 Kr
37 Rb	38 Sr	39 Y	40 Zr	41 Nb	42 Mo	43 Tc	44 Ru	45 Rh	46 Pd	47 Ag	48 Cd	49 In	50 Sn	51 Sb	52 Te	53 I	54 Xe
55 Cs	56 Ba		72 Hf	73 Ta	74 W	75 Re	76 Os	77 Ir	78 Pt	79 Au	80 Hg	81 Tl	82 Pb	83 Bi	84 Po	85 At	86 Rn
87 Fr	88 Ra		104 Rf	105 Db	106 Sg	107 Bh	108 Hs	109 Mt	110 Ds	111 Rg	112 Cn	113 Nh	114 Fl	115 Mc	116 Lv	117 Ts	118 Og

57 La	58 Ce	59 Pr	60 Nd	61 Pm	62 Sm	63 Eu	64 Gd	65 Tb	66 Dy	67 Ho	68 Er	69 Tm	70 Yb	71 Lu
89 Ac	90 Th	91 Pa	92 U	93 Np	94 Pu	95 Am	96 Cm	97 Bk	98 Cf	99 Es	100 Fm	101 Md	102 No	103 Lr

The halogens (group 17 of the periodic table) share many properties, largely because of their position way to the right of the table. All of them react easily with other elements, aiming to complete their octet of eight outer electrons. They also combine with hydrogen to make strong acids; simple salts can be made from those acids. And that leads right back to the name halogen, which comes from two Greek words meaning "salt producer."

DANGER LEVEL

☢️ ☢️ ☢️ ☢️

There's no doubt that fluorine is *very* dangerous, but fortunately you won't find it in your backyard. You might, however, find it somewhere even closer — in the water you drink. Fierce debates rage about whether fluorine is a life (or tooth) saver . . . or a public-health menace.

EXPERIMENT *with the* ELEMENT

OK, so you've heard all about fluoride helping protect your teeth, but how does it do that? And what would happen if you didn't use it? The next experiment might just tell you.

TRY THE FLUORINE TOOTH TEST

Cavities form when the enamel (the outer layer) of a tooth is eaten away by acids in the mouth. That acid builds up when bacteria in the mouth start to digest food on the surface of the tooth. (Bet you didn't know you have acid in your mouth!) This experiment uses an eggshell to represent your tooth. Why? Because the surface of the eggshell, like that of a tooth, contains a lot of enamel. And instead of some bacteria-produced acid, you're using a natural acid sitting right in the kitchen cupboard—vinegar.

YOU WILL NEED

- ◆ **2 eggs**
- ◆ **3 drinking glasses (about 1 cup (250 ml) size or slightly larger)**
- ◆ **Fluoride rinse (such as Colgate Phos-Flur or ACT Anticavity Fluoride Rinse)**
- ◆ **White vinegar**

METHOD

1. Put an egg in one of the glasses and fill the glass with fluoride rinse until the egg is covered.

2 Pour the same amount of vinegar into the other two glasses.

3 Wait 10 minutes and then put the "fluoride egg" in one of the two vinegar glasses.

4 Put the other egg in the second vinegar glass.

5 Observe what happens to each egg.

HEY, WHAT'S GOING ON?

The "fluoride egg" might have one or two bubbles on it, but the other egg will be bubbling away quickly. That's because the acid in the vinegar is eating away at the minerals in the surface of the eggshell, but the fluoride is protecting its egg from contact with the acid. How? By strengthening the crystals of the enamel and making them more resistant to acid attack. Fluoride in toothpaste (or drinking water) is also attracted to the enamel surface of your teeth, and it then attracts more minerals—including more of the calcium that is an important enamel ingredient. These extra mineral layers protect against acid.

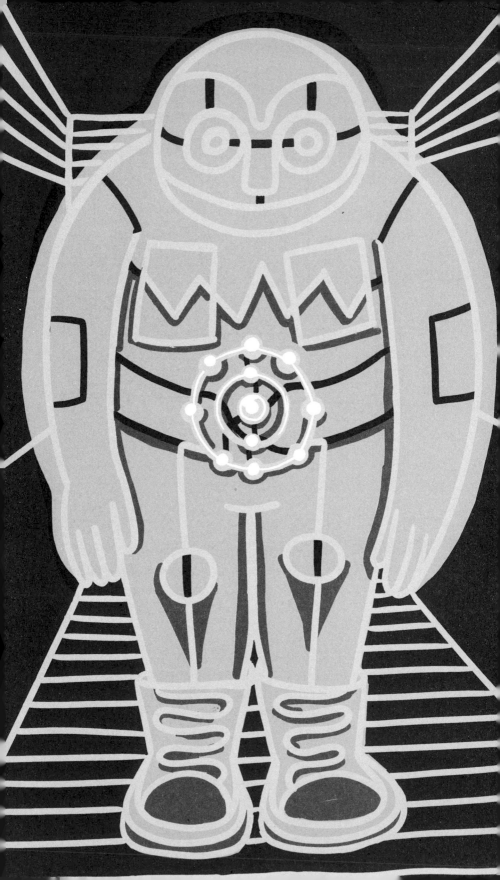

ATOMIC NUMBER: 10	ELECTRONS IN OUTERMOST SHELL: 8
ATOMIC WEIGHT: 20.1797	MELTING POINT: -415.46°F (-248.59°C)
ELEMENT SYMBOL: Ne	BOILING POINT: -410.88°F (-246.05°C)

CHAPTER 8

NEON

¹H																	²He
³Li	⁴Be											⁵B	⁶C	⁷N	⁸O	⁹F	¹⁰Ne
¹¹Na	¹²Mg											¹³Al	¹⁴Si	¹⁵P	¹⁶S	¹⁷Cl	¹⁸Ar
¹⁹K	²⁰Ca	²¹Sc	²²Ti	²³V	²⁴Cr	²⁵Mn	²⁶Fe	²⁷Co	²⁸Ni	²⁹Cu	³⁰Zn	³¹Ga	³²Ge	³³As	³⁴Se	³⁵Br	³⁶Kr
³⁷Rb	³⁸Sr	³⁹Y	⁴⁰Zr	⁴¹Nb	⁴²Mo	⁴³Tc	⁴⁴Ru	⁴⁵Rh	⁴⁶Pd	⁴⁷Ag	⁴⁸Cd	⁴⁹In	⁵⁰Sn	⁵¹Sb	⁵²Te	⁵³I	⁵⁴Xe
⁵⁵Cs	⁵⁶Ba		⁷²Hf	⁷³Ta	⁷⁴W	⁷⁵Re	⁷⁶Os	⁷⁷Ir	⁷⁸Pt	⁷⁹Au	⁸⁰Hg	⁸¹Tl	⁸²Pb	⁸³Bi	⁸⁴Po	⁸⁵At	⁸⁶Rn
⁸⁷Fr	⁸⁸Ra		¹⁰⁴Rf	¹⁰⁵Db	¹⁰⁶Sg	¹⁰⁷Bh	¹⁰⁸Hs	¹⁰⁹Mt	¹¹⁰Ds	¹¹¹Rg	¹¹²Cn	¹¹³Nh	¹¹⁴Fl	¹¹⁵Mc	¹¹⁶Lv	¹¹⁷Ts	¹¹⁸Og

	⁵⁷La	⁵⁸Ce	⁵⁹Pr	⁶⁰Nd	⁶¹Pm	⁶²Sm	⁶³Eu	⁶⁴Gd	⁶⁵Tb	⁶⁶Dy	⁶⁷Ho	⁶⁸Er	⁶⁹Tm	⁷⁰Yb	⁷¹Lu
	⁸⁹Ac	⁹⁰Th	⁹¹Pa	⁹²U	⁹³Np	⁹⁴Pu	⁹⁵Am	⁹⁶Cm	⁹⁷Bk	⁹⁸Cf	⁹⁹Es	¹⁰⁰Fm	¹⁰¹Md	¹⁰²No	¹⁰³Lr

Go ahead, think of the word "neon"—what sort of images spring to mind? How about colorfully lit restaurants and hotels in Las Vegas, Chicago, Tokyo, or New York? Most of us know neon for its use in colored lights. That element must really be pretty reactive to get results like that, right? Well, not really—neon is actually one of the least reactive elements and a good example of the "no reactions for me" behavior of the noble gas group of elements. But that hasn't stopped neon from having a long and vivid relationship with humans—from the ancient Greeks to 17th-century labs to colorful motel signs in the Nevada desert.

WHAT DOES NEON LOOK LIKE?

Neon is an odorless, colorless gas at the sort of temperatures we prefer. Things would have to get *pretty* cold—down by a few hundred degrees—for you to see it as a liquid. Its position at the right-hand edge of the periodic table identifies it as a noble gas, so you're not going to see much change in appearance if neon reacts with another element. Because it can't and won't.

Of course, neon *is* famous for its appearance—a bright reddish-orange that appears when an electric current passes through the neon gas. And it's that same color when it's used in neon lights. The electricity "excites" some of the neon electrons, causing them to move into a different energy state. When they return to their normal state, they release the extra energy in the form of light particles called photons.

WHEN WAS NEON DISCOVERED?

Let's face it, you're not going to find a lot of an inert (doesn't react with anything) gas too easily. One of the few places where it exists naturally is in the air, and even there it makes up only about 0.03 percent of the total. How do we know that? Well, it's a long story—or perhaps we should say it's a story that goes a long way back.

People have always noticed the air around them. After all, it's everywhere! We breathe it in and exhale it, so even the most primitive people must have realized its importance—particularly if they held their breath or were underwater. The ancient Greeks, for instance, tried to define the world around them scientifically. They decided that there were four elements: Earth, Air, Fire, and Water.

That's pretty much how it remained for nearly 3,000 years, until the 17th century. That's when scientists developed the instruments and techniques to study materials (including gases such as air) precisely. They observed that something in the air helped things burn (oxygen), but that air contained other gases too (nitrogen and carbon dioxide). Over the next 250 years, they became even more precise, and by the end of the 17th century, scientists had accounted for 99.966 percent of what made up air.

If you got 99.966 percent on a quiz, you'd probably get pretty excited, right? Well, that's not how scientists look at things. That missing 0.034 percent really bugged them. Just what the heck was it? In the 1890s, British chemists William Ramsay and Morris Travers used the new technique of examining spectra to see whether the mystery would be solved. They discovered argon (atomic number 18), but then became convinced that something must lie in the same column of the periodic table, above argon and below helium. See how they were following the logic of Mendeleev when he left blanks (see page 37)?

Morris Travers and William Ramsay

After lengthy studies of cooling air to liquid form and then boiling it and observing spectral lines, Ramsay and Travers finally had a flash of discovery in 1898. And they got more than they bargained for: a new element. The gas even *glowed* in a dramatic scarlet color. Ramsay later recalled:

> *For the moment the actual spectrum of the gas did not matter in the least, for nothing in the world gave a glow such as we had seen.*

His son Willie suggested calling the new element *novum* (Latin for "new"), but Dad chose the Greek word instead—neon.

WHERE IS NEON USED?

The neon in those lights only produces a reddish-orange glow. Lighting engineers need to add traces of other elements (such as mercury or krypton) to get a wider range of colors in their "neon signs."

Neon is also used in lasers, television tubes, and vacuum tubes. Its lack of reactivity means that it forms

an effective shield around delicate objects such as wires that could be damaged or contaminated if they came into contact with oxygen or other gases, for example, through oxidation (see page 56).

In addition to being a contender for the "least reactive element" award, neon has the narrowest liquid range of any element. Less than five degrees Fahrenheit separate neon's boiling point from its freezing point, and that narrow "window of opportunity" is surprisingly important. Liquid neon can be used as a refrigerant (something that cools other things, like your refrigerator), and it's said to be 40 times more effective 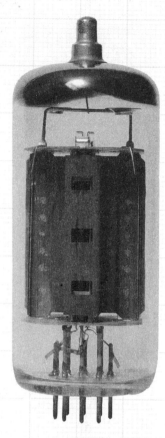 than liquid helium and three times more effective than hydrogen. Who knew it was neon helping to keep your leftovers cold?

Meet the Relatives

GROUP 18: NOT SO NOBLE?

1 H																	2 He
3 Li	4 Be											5 B	6 C	7 N	8 O	9 F	10 Ne
11 Na	12 Mg											13 Al	14 Si	15 P	16 S	17 Cl	18 Ar
19 K	20 Ca	21 Sc	22 Ti	23 V	24 Cr	25 Mn	26 Fe	27 Co	28 Ni	29 Cu	30 Zn	31 Ga	32 Ge	33 As	34 Se	35 Br	36 Kr
37 Rb	38 Sr	39 Y	40 Zr	41 Nb	42 Mo	43 Tc	44 Ru	45 Rh	46 Pd	47 Ag	48 Cd	49 In	50 Sn	51 Sb	52 Te	53 I	54 Xe
55 Cs	56 Ba		72 Hf	73 Ta	74 W	75 Re	76 Os	77 Ir	78 Pt	79 Au	80 Hg	81 Tl	82 Pb	83 Bi	84 Po	85 At	86 Rn
87 Fr	88 Ra		104 Rf	105 Db	106 Sg	107 Bh	108 Hs	109 Mt	110 Ds	111 Rg	112 Cn	113 Nh	114 Fl	115 Mc	116 Lv	117 Ts	118 Og

57 La	58 Ce	59 Pr	60 Nd	61 Pm	62 Sm	63 Eu	64 Gd	65 Tb	66 Dy	67 Ho	68 Er	69 Tm	70 Yb	71 Lu
89 Ac	90 Th	91 Pa	92 U	93 Np	94 Pu	95 Am	96 Cm	97 Bk	98 Cf	99 Es	100 Fm	101 Md	102 No	103 Lr

The elements in group 18 of the periodic table, the noble gases, have always been considered unable to bond with other elements. That was certainly true in the days when these elements were first observed. Using sophisticated lab techniques, however, scientists have now been able to form compounds with a number of neon's relatives. Some of the noble elements have formed compounds with oxygen, fluorine, and hydrogen. And some of the applications might make the effort pay off: These compounds are excellent at nabbing electrons from nearby elements, making them useful in dozens of chemical reactions.

DANGER LEVEL

There's very little you can do with neon to make it dangerous. Compared with sodium, the explosive element next to it in the periodic table, neon might appear to be a bit dull. About the only bad thing that might happen — and you'd have to be in a high-tech lab for this to occur — would be if liquid neon came in contact with your skin. The result would be severe frostbite!

EXPERIMENT *with the* ELEMENT

For many years, neon and other elements in its group were called "inert gases" because they would never react with other elements. Well, some chemists weren't so sure about that and managed to form new compounds using them (as we saw earlier in the "Meet the Relatives" section). What's more, the word "inert" really suggests a complete lack of activity, and that's just not the case with the noble gases. Even if an element such as neon isn't reacting with another element, it can behave in all kinds of ways in all kinds of circumstances—as you'll see in the next illuminating experiment.

EVEN NEON GETS EXCITED

Noble elements are supposed be inert, or incapable of reacting with other things. But neon's ability to bloom in bright colors shows that even this "inert" element can get excited with a little input in the form of electricity. You might already have some colorful neon lamps or even a color-activated voltage tester laying around the house to use in this experiment. No? Don't worry—you can use a fluorescent light bulb instead. Sure, it's filled with a different gas (mercury vapor), but the experiment gets the same result.

YOU WILL NEED

- ◆ **Neon (or fluorescent) bulb**
- ◆ **Popsicle stick**
- ◆ **Copper tape**
- ◆ **Carpeted floor**
- ◆ **Wool socks to wear**
- ◆ **Metal doorknob or hinge**

WARNING! Make sure you have an adult handling the bulb.

METHOD

1 Attach the bulb to the end of the Popsicle stick with the copper tape.

2 Wrap the tape around the stick several more times.

3 Hold the stick upright, with your fingers pinching the taped part.

4 Put on the socks and scuff your feet along the floor.

5 Touch the copper tape of the stick to the metal doorknob and watch the bulb light up.

HEY, WHAT'S GOING ON?

If you've ever stuck a balloon to the wall after rubbing it against a sweater, you'll know the awesome power of static electricity. It's the flow of electrons from one object to another. Here you're doing the same thing, except you are transferring the electrons to the neon light. All that sock-scuffing rubbed electrons off the wool, making you positively charged. Touching the knob let lots of negatively charged electrons flow through the copper tape into you and the bulb. The arrival of these electrons "excites" the electrons of the neon atoms, causing them to emit light as they return to their original energy levels.

ATOMIC NUMBER: 11	ELECTRONS IN OUTERMOST SHELL: 1
ATOMIC WEIGHT: 22.9898	MELTING POINT: 207.9°F (97.79°C)
ELEMENT SYMBOL: Na	BOILING POINT: 1,621.29°F (882.94°C)

CHAPTER 9

SODIUM

1 H																	2 He
3 Li	4 Be											5 B	6 C	7 N	8 O	9 F	10 Ne
11 Na	12 Mg											13 Al	14 Si	15 P	16 S	17 Cl	18 Ar
19 K	20 Ca	21 Sc	22 Ti	23 V	24 Cr	25 Mn	26 Fe	27 Co	28 Ni	29 Cu	30 Zn	31 Ga	32 Ge	33 As	34 Se	35 Br	36 Kr
37 Rb	38 Sr	39 Y	40 Zr	41 Nb	42 Mo	43 Tc	44 Ru	45 Rh	46 Pd	47 Ag	48 Cd	49 In	50 Sn	51 Sb	52 Te	53 I	54 Xe
55 Cs	56 Ba		72 Hf	73 Ta	74 W	75 Re	76 Os	77 Ir	78 Pt	79 Au	80 Hg	81 Tl	82 Pb	83 Bi	84 Po	85 At	86 Rn
87 Fr	88 Ra		104 Rf	105 Db	106 Sg	107 Bh	108 Hs	109 Mt	110 Ds	111 Rg	112 Cn	113 Nh	114 Fl	115 Mc	116 Lv	117 Ts	118 Og

57 La	58 Ce	59 Pr	60 Nd	61 Pm	62 Sm	63 Eu	64 Gd	65 Tb	66 Dy	67 Ho	68 Er	69 Tm	70 Yb	71 Lu
89 Ac	90 Th	91 Pa	92 U	93 Np	94 Pu	95 Am	96 Cm	97 Bk	98 Cf	99 Es	100 Fm	101 Md	102 No	103 Lr

"**P**ass the salt, please—this chicken is tasteless. Oh, and a glass of water, because salty food always makes me thirsty."

Ka-BOOM!!!

"Whoops—that might've been *pure* sodium, and I meant to give him salt. Oh, well . . . win some, lose some."

OK, with that completely made-up exchange, you will have learned a very important thing about sodium: It seems to combine with water in explosive ways.

WHAT DOES SODIUM LOOK LIKE?

Pure sodium is a soft and silvery metal—so soft that you could cut it with the edge of a coin. And if you did cut a piece of sodium, the surface would start to turn duller. That's because the sodium would react with the oxygen in the air—a process called oxidation. (Rust forming on iron or a slice of apple turning brown are also examples of oxidation.)

Sodium has a low density, meaning that a given volume of sodium doesn't weigh very much. In fact, it is less dense than water and would float on it . . . if it didn't react violently when it hit the water. With its single free electron, it's always ready to react quickly, and the reaction with water releases heat energy as well as hydrogen—and we all know how flammable hydrogen is.

Sodium is one of those elements (most of the elements, in fact) that aren't found in their pure state in nature. The reason why should be pretty clear when you look at its position on the periodic table. There it is on the far left, in column 1—that means it has one electron in its outer shell. But in the same way that the halogens over there in column 17 are looking to get just one electron to *fill* their outer shell, sodium is always trying to *get rid of* one electron to empty its shell.

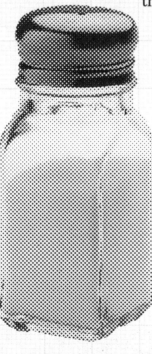

All of this is to say that sodium forms all sorts of compounds, and human beings have known those compounds for thousands of years. The most widely known is, of course, salt—a simple compound of sodium giving away its spare electron to chlorine, which needs just one. Simple: sodium chloride (NaCl).

WHEN WAS SODIUM DISCOVERED?

By the early 19th century, scientists were experimenting with new ways of discovering pure elements, usually by working with materials that they felt certain were compounds of different elements. Sir Humphry Davy (how many times does *his* name crop up in this book?) had concluded that the bonds that held different elements together in compounds were electrical—and we know now that electricity describes the flow of electrons.

In 1807, Davy worked on a hot sample of a familiar substance, caustic soda (sodium hydroxide), using a method known as electrolysis. He ran an electrical charge through the caustic soda to break it into its component parts. A silvery liquid emerged and slowly cooled to become a soft solid. Davy named this new element sodium in honor of the caustic soda that he had used. The German word for caustic soda is *natronlauge*, which is why sodium's chemical abbreviation is Na.

Sir Humphry Davy

WHERE IS SODIUM USED?

That simple sodium chloride compound has another name: table salt. And although having too much of it can lead to heart disease and other illnesses—not to mention a serious need for a glass of water—salt really is a necessity for human beings. Just think of some of those expressions: "He's really worth his salt" or "She's the salt of the earth." Even our word "salary" comes from the Latin word *salarium*, which was a payment that Roman soldiers received to buy salt.

Ancient people first knew of sodium through one of its compounds, sodium carbonate (Na_2CO_3), which the Egyptians called *natron*. They used it to dry and preserve dead bodies before turning them into mummies. The Romans called that same compound *natrium* (that abbreviation Na for the element is looking a little less weird). Centuries ago, the Arabs also used sodium carbonate, but called it *suda* ("headache") because they believed it cured headaches.

Pure sodium, in its liquid form, plays an important role in nuclear power plants. It acts as a heat exchange, absorbing some of the enormous heat produced in the atomic reactions and flowing through pipes into a room full of water. The extreme heat turns the water to steam, which operates machines that generate electricity.

Most of sodium's usefulness comes from its many compounds. Table salt, or sodium chloride, has many uses in cooking and beyond. That simple compound is also a chemical first step to producing many other sodium compounds that are used in medicine, cooking, and industry. Nearly all of these are soluble (they dissolve well) in water: Just think of adding salt to the water for cooking pasta or watching when your grandpa stirs some bicarbonate of soda into water to help cure an upset stomach. And, of course, there must be a reason why people put salt on food. One theory is that the sodium in the salt reacts with chemicals in your tongue's taste buds, making them more efficient at sending taste signals to the brain.

SOLUBLE

Able to dissolve into (or become part of) another substance. A substance that dissolves, like salt or sugar, is called a solute. The substance that it dissolves into, like water or coffee, is called the solvent. Once the solute dissolves into the solvent, the resulting mix is called a solution.

Meet the Relatives

GROUP 1: ALKALI METALS

1 H																	2 He
3 Li	4 Be											5 B	6 C	7 N	8 O	9 F	10 Ne
11 Na	12 Mg											13 Al	14 Si	15 P	16 S	17 Cl	18 Ar
19 K	20 Ca	21 Sc	22 Ti	23 V	24 Cr	25 Mn	26 Fe	27 Co	28 Ni	29 Cu	30 Zn	31 Ga	32 Ge	33 As	34 Se	35 Br	36 Kr
37 Rb	38 Sr	39 Y	40 Zr	41 Nb	42 Mo	43 Tc	44 Ru	45 Rh	46 Pd	47 Ag	48 Cd	49 In	50 Sn	51 Sb	52 Te	53 I	54 Xe
55 Cs	56 Ba		72 Hf	73 Ta	74 W	75 Re	76 Os	77 Ir	78 Pt	79 Au	80 Hg	81 Tl	82 Pb	83 Bi	84 Po	85 At	86 Rn
87 Fr	88 Ra		104 Rf	105 Db	106 Sg	107 Bh	108 Hs	109 Mt	110 Ds	111 Rg	112 Cn	113 Nh	114 Fl	115 Mc	116 Lv	117 Ts	118 Og

57 La	58 Ce	59 Pr	60 Nd	61 Pm	62 Sm	63 Eu	64 Gd	65 Tb	66 Dy	67 Ho	68 Er	69 Tm	70 Yb	71 Lu
89 Ac	90 Th	91 Pa	92 U	93 Np	94 Pu	95 Am	96 Cm	97 Bk	98 Cf	99 Es	100 Fm	101 Md	102 No	103 Lr

All the elements in sodium's column of the periodic table (except hydrogen) are called alkali metals. None of these soft metals occurs freely in nature, probably because they are all such highly reactive elements. They can easily lose their single valence electron in reactions with other elements, and some of those reactions (especially with water) can be explosive. The farther down the table you go, the more explosive these alkali metals get—cesium (Cs) and francium (Fr) are highly reactive. The reaction between cesium and water is particularly violent and explosive. It produces cesium hydroxide, which is the strongest base (see page 103) known. It's strong enough to eat through glass.

As you can imagine, any element that reacts violently with water will be pretty dangerous to be around. (Have you noticed all the water on this planet?!) That's pure sodium, but some of its compounds, such as sodium hydroxide, can cause serious burns if people come into contact with them.

We also hear about the health risks of too much "sodium" in people's diets. What the people really mean is table salt, or sodium chloride, which is our main source of sodium. Our bodies do need some sodium to function properly, but too much can damage nerves and limit our ability to digest fats. The most likely risk of too much salt is the link to high blood pressure, which increases the risk of heart disease and stroke.

EXPERIMENT *with the* ELEMENT

Sodium crops up in all sorts of ways—perhaps one of the most surprising is its role in the production of "hot ice." What's that? Make some and see.

HOT ICE

This is an experiment with a bizarre result—an "ice" that's hot. The solid ice owes more to its crystal structure than to any real cold, but it's still astonishing. What you'll produce is actually the chemical sodium acetate, which is an amazingly helpful ingredient in industry, food preparation, and water purification. Not to mention its use as a seat warmer at football games or a hand warmer for snowboarding.

YOU WILL NEED

- **4 cups (1 liter) of white vinegar**
- **Saucepan**
- **Stove**
- **4 tablespoons (45 ml) of baking soda**
- **Mixing bowl (nonplastic)**
- **Plastic wrap**
- **Shallow dish or dinner plate**
- **Refrigerator**

WARNING! Make sure an adult is present at all times and supervises the cooking and pouring.

METHOD

1 Pour the vinegar into the saucepan and place it on the stove with the heat off.

2 Add the baking soda to the vinegar slowly, stirring after each addition.

3 When it is all mixed in, turn on the heat and bring the liquid to a boil without stirring.

4 Continue boiling over medium heat until a crystal film starts to form on the surface. (This could take more than 45 minutes, so be patient.)

5 Pour the liquid into the mixing bowl and cover with the plastic wrap.

6 Put the mixing bowl in the refrigerator for two hours.

7. Pour the liquid into the shallow dish. It should immediately "freeze" into crystals.

8. If it does not, scrape a crystal from the mixing bowl and drop it into the liquid to trigger a freeze.

HEY, WHAT'S GOING ON?

Mixing and heating the vinegar and baking soda is actually a chemical reaction that produces sodium acetate (in liquid form) and carbon dioxide gas. The liquid sodium acetate crystallizes instantly when it is disturbed, turning solid. Although this isn't "ice" as we know it, the reaction to create it is exothermic, meaning that it gives off heat. That's why sodium acetate is used in those seat and hand warmers that get hot when you crunch them. Water freezing also gives off heat, which is why orange growers spray their orchards with water if they fear a frost.

ATOMIC NUMBER: 12	ELECTRONS IN OUTERMOST SHELL: 2
ATOMIC WEIGHT: 24.3050	MELTING POINT: 1,202°F (650°C)
ELEMENT SYMBOL: Mg	BOILING POINT: 1,994°F (1,090°C)

CHAPTER 10

MAGNESIUM

1 H																	2 He
3 Li	4 Be											5 B	6 C	7 N	8 O	9 F	10 Ne
11 Na	12 Mg											13 Al	14 Si	15 P	16 S	17 Cl	18 Ar
19 K	20 Ca	21 Sc	22 Ti	23 V	24 Cr	25 Mn	26 Fe	27 Co	28 Ni	29 Cu	30 Zn	31 Ga	32 Ge	33 As	34 Se	35 Br	36 Kr
37 Rb	38 Sr	39 Y	40 Zr	41 Nb	42 Mo	43 Tc	44 Ru	45 Rh	46 Pd	47 Ag	48 Cd	49 In	50 Sn	51 Sb	52 Te	53 I	54 Xe
55 Cs	56 Ba		72 Hf	73 Ta	74 W	75 Re	76 Os	77 Ir	78 Pt	79 Au	80 Hg	81 Tl	82 Pb	83 Bi	84 Po	85 At	86 Rn
87 Fr	88 Ra		104 Rf	105 Db	106 Sg	107 Bh	108 Hs	109 Mt	110 Ds	111 Rg	112 Cn	113 Nh	114 Fl	115 Mc	116 Lv	117 Ts	118 Og

57 La	58 Ce	59 Pr	60 Nd	61 Pm	62 Sm	63 Eu	64 Gd	65 Tb	66 Dy	67 Ho	68 Er	69 Tm	70 Yb	71 Lu
89 Ac	90 Th	91 Pa	92 U	93 Np	94 Pu	95 Am	96 Cm	97 Bk	98 Cf	99 Es	100 Fm	101 Md	102 No	103 Lr

An ingredient of aircraft and trucks that is lightweight and durable. An element with links to the distant past, a world of magnetism, and mysterious forces. A must-have for humans and plants alike. Is there anything that magnesium can't do? Maybe, but it's so capable of bonding with other elements that people keep coming up with new uses for this "blast from the past." Wanna get a reaction out of someone or something? You might want to try magnesium first.

WHAT DOES MAGNESIUM LOOK LIKE?

Magnesium is a silvery-white metal that is considerably harder than one of its next-door neighbors on the periodic table, sodium (atomic number 11), but not as strong as its neighbor on the other side, aluminum (atomic number 13). It's rare to find pure magnesium, because it reacts easily with other elements to form compounds. Even a chunk of pure magnesium soon tarnishes (loses its shine because of a chemical reaction) when exposed to air. That's because it reacts with the oxygen in the air in a process called oxidation.

WHEN WAS MAGNESIUM DISCOVERED?

As with lots of elements, people knew about magnesium indirectly for thousands of years before they recognized it as an element in its own right. The name "magnesium" is a clue to this fascinating history. Things go waaaay back about 2,500 years to a region in eastern Greece that was then called Magnesia. (Hmm . . . maybe related?) Local people identified two metal ores—one black and one white—and called them both "magnesia."

Over time, people noticed that these two ores had a lot more differences than just color. In fact, one version of the black ore attracted metals—and that gave us the word "magnet." Eventually chemists recognized that there were two elements behind this pair of ores. In time scientists identified the element manganese (Mn) as one of the sources of the black ores.

We now know that the white ores, which took on the name "magnesia," were compounds of magnesium and various other elements. The story moves on to Epsom, a town in southern England, in the year 1618. Farmer Henry Wicker led some of his cows to a well during a

severe drought. But despite the heat and dry conditions, the cows refused to drink. Wicker tasted the water and found it bitter. Being something of a scientist himself, Farmer Wicker boiled some of the water and collected the powder that remained. He soon noticed that the powder healed cuts and rashes ... and before long it became clear that the powder also helped cure constipation (ask your parents about that one). This mysterious powder was in fact the compound magnesium sulfate (magnesium plus sulfur and oxygen), but even now many people still know it by the name it took on as a medicine—Epsom salts.

Wicker might have been happy enough to know that he had produced a powder with curative powers. But the 17th and 18th centuries also saw the beginning of modern scientific inquiry. In 1755, Scottish chemist Joseph Black announced a new element even though he wasn't able to isolate a sample of it. Fifty-three years later, Sir Humphry Davy isolated some of it using electrolysis. He first called it "magnium," but later settled for the name "magnesium."

WHERE IS MAGNESIUM USED?

Magnesium reacts easily with many other elements, and its compounds have many uses. One of the most important derives from its combination with aluminum—the resulting alloy is known for its strength and is used to produce ships, truck and train bodies, and chemical tankers.

The real importance of magnesium, though, comes from the many roles it plays in nature. Magnesium is a key ingredient in chlorophyll, the molecule that enables plants to draw energy from sunlight in the process called photosynthesis. Farmers and gardeners can easily identify plants and trees that suffer from magnesium deficiency—the normally green leaves take on a sickly yellowish color. It won't come as a surprise, then, that magnesium is an ingredient in many fertilizers.

ALLOY

A metal made by combining two or more metallic elements.

Humans also need magnesium, and we get it either directly from plants or from animals that eat plants. Our bodies use magnesium in hundreds of ways, such as regulating blood sugar and preventing strokes and heart attacks.

Meet the Relatives

GROUP 2: ALKALINE EARTH METALS

1 H																	2 He
3 Li	4 Be											5 B	6 C	7 N	8 O	9 F	10 Ne
11 Na	12 Mg											13 Al	14 Si	15 P	16 S	17 Cl	18 Ar
19 K	20 Ca	21 Sc	22 Ti	23 V	24 Cr	25 Mn	26 Fe	27 Co	28 Ni	29 Cu	30 Zn	31 Ga	32 Ge	33 As	34 Se	35 Br	36 Kr
37 Rb	38 Sr	39 Y	40 Zr	41 Nb	42 Mo	43 Tc	44 Ru	45 Rh	46 Pd	47 Ag	48 Cd	49 In	50 Sn	51 Sb	52 Te	53 I	54 Xe
55 Cs	56 Ba		72 Hf	73 Ta	74 W	75 Re	76 Os	77 Ir	78 Pt	79 Au	80 Hg	81 Tl	82 Pb	83 Bi	84 Po	85 At	86 Rn
87 Fr	88 Ra		104 Rf	105 Db	106 Sg	107 Bh	108 Hs	109 Mt	110 Ds	111 Rg	112 Cn	113 Nh	114 Fl	115 Mc	116 Lv	117 Ts	118 Og

57 La	58 Ce	59 Pr	60 Nd	61 Pm	62 Sm	63 Eu	64 Gd	65 Tb	66 Dy	67 Ho	68 Er	69 Tm	70 Yb	71 Lu
89 Ac	90 Th	91 Pa	92 U	93 Np	94 Pu	95 Am	96 Cm	97 Bk	98 Cf	99 Es	100 Fm	101 Md	102 No	103 Lr

The elements in the second column of the periodic table are known as the alkaline earth metals. Like magnesium, they have two valence (outer shell) electrons, which they can lose easily when they react with other elements. All of these elements are common in nature (even if they're usually found in compounds). They are silver-colored and soft—at least compared to other metals.

What's up with those names—"alkaline" and "earth?" Well, "alkaline" describes the result when something releases a positive hydrogen ion (H⁺) when dissolved in water. It is sometimes called a base. An acid, on the other hand, produces a negative hydroxide ion (OH⁻) in the same circumstances. Strong bases and acids are powerful enough to corrode (weaken or destroy) other materials: Think of drain cleaner or bleach (both are bases) or warnings about touching battery acid.

Meanwhile, "earth" is an old-fashioned term for something that doesn't dissolve in water and is heat-resistant.

DANGER LEVEL

Magnesium's quickness to react means that it is highly flammable, so people should always take care when dealing with it. Without enough precautions, it can cause serious injury — or worse. In 1955, a racing car built of magnesium crashed in the famous Le Mans 24-hour race in France. The accident killed 83 spectators plus the driver — many of the deaths and injuries were caused by bits of flying magnesium, which had ignited because of a fire in the fuel tank. Although magnesium's flammability poses a risk, it is also a feature that people have put to use over the years. The first photographic flashes were created when photographers lit magnesium powder or ribbons with a match or a candle.

EXPERIMENT *with the* ELEMENT

The next two experiments offer a contrast. The first, as its name suggests, is more of a trick than an experiment. But the difference is that you'll be able to explain the science of why it works when you've finished. The second is just as much fun, and it throws in a bit of scientific history—well, it uses Epsom salts, which played such a big role in the history of the element.

TRICK BIRTHDAY CANDLES

If you've never seen trick birthday candles, then you're in for a treat. Just like a prop from a slapstick movie, these candles seem normal as they burn on a cake. Then the birthday boy or girl makes a wish, blows the candles out . . . and they light up again! How did that happen?!

Well, you don't have to mix much or do much preparation for this one—apart from heading to a party store or joke shop to stock up on candles. Just read the science bit at the end so you can explain the trick to your audience. Of course, the best time to do this trick is at the birthday of one of your friends or relatives. Make sure to get an adult in on the secret so you'll have some help.

YOU WILL NEED

- ◆ **Trick candles (birthday cake size)**
- ◆ **Birthday cake or some cupcakes**
- ◆ **Matches**

MATCH ALERT!

Also, make sure an adult disposes of the candles safely, running them under cold water until they're absolutely extinguished.

METHOD

1 Fit about nine candles in the cake or three each in three cupcakes.

2 Tell your friend that you've made a special birthday cake, and show them the cake you've prepared.

3 With an adult's supervision, use the matches to light the candles.

4 Get the friend to make a wish and then blow the candles out.

5 While everyone claps, watch as the candles magically light themselves again.

6 See whether your friend can blow them out this time.

7 Get an adult to take the candles away, but only after you promise to explain what happened.

HEY, WHAT'S GOING ON?

When you blow out a normal candle, you'll see a little smoke rising from the wick. That's vaporized candle wax. The glowing ember of the wick is still warm enough to vaporize the candle wax, but not hot enough to reignite.

The wicks of trick candles have been treated with magnesium flakes. This time, when the candle is blown out, the ember isn't hot enough to ignite the wax vapor, but it *is* hot enough to light the magnesium, which ignites at a temperature of about 800°F. And the magnesium, in turn, burns at a temperature that's hot enough to ignite that vaporized candle wax.

CRACKPOT CRYSTALS

Don't you just love crystals? Many of the elements in the periodic table are crystals or can form crystals—from the everyday (table salt, or sodium chloride) to the very expensive (diamonds, or pure carbon). But magnesium sulfate, or good old Epsom salts, can be harnessed to make amazing spiky crystals in no time at all. And with a little planning, you can add a dash of real color to the results.

YOU WILL NEED

- ◆ **Half cup (120 ml) of Epsom salts**
- ◆ **Half cup (120 ml) of hot water (from the faucet—no need to boil it)**
- ◆ **Small mixing bowl**
- ◆ **Wooden mixing spoon**
- ◆ **Food coloring**

WARNING! Hot water!

METHOD

1 Combine the Epsom salts with the water in the mixing bowl.

2 Stir with the spoon until the salt has been dissolved (a little can remain).

3 Add a few drops of food coloring and stir.

4 Put the mixing bowl in the refrigerator.

5 Remove after three hours, and marvel at the crystals you've produced.

HEY, WHAT'S GOING ON?

Epsom salts, or magnesium sulfate ($MgSO_4$), dissolve easily in the hot water because the water molecules become more active and move faster as they warm up, colliding and reacting with the Epsom salt molecules more rapidly. As the water cools in the refrigerator, it can't hold as many of the Epsom salts dissolved in it because the gaps between the cooler water molecules have become smaller. The magnesium sulfate atoms are forced out of the solution and join together in the long, narrow crystal shapes you see in the bowl—and growing out of it.

ATOMIC NUMBER: 13	ELECTRONS IN OUTERMOST SHELL: 3
ATOMIC WEIGHT: 26.9816	MELTING POINT: 1,220.58°F (660.32°C)
ELEMENT SYMBOL: Al	BOILING POINT: 4,566°F (2,519°C)

CHAPTER 11

ALUMINUM

If you're lucky enough to live in a state with cash refunds for bottle deposits, recycling aluminum cans is a great way to earn some quick cash. Aluminum is undoubtedly one of the most useful elements going, and there's more of it in the Earth's crust than any other element. Yet it's really hard to extract it from its ore, bauxite. In fact, those empty cans start to look like pretty good value when you realize that it takes 20 times more energy to extract pure aluminum from its ore than it does to recycle it. But even at 20 times the cost, aluminum seems worth it. After all, it's used in everything from soda cans and food packaging to baseball bats, power lines, rocket fuel, and ships' masts.

WHAT DOES ALUMINUM LOOK LIKE?

In its natural state, aluminum is a soft and malleable (easily bent or twisted) metal. Despite being so common, aluminum is very rare in its pure form. Two main reasons tell you why. First, aluminum atoms are locked very tightly in the molecules of bauxite, the most common aluminum ore (although it's found in about 270 other minerals).

The second reason also sheds light on one of aluminum's big pluses. Aluminum oxidizes (reacts with oxygen) as soon as it is exposed to air. But unlike destructive forms of oxidation (think of a rusty old playground swing), aluminum's oxidation turns out to be protective. The reaction leaves the surface of the aluminum covered with a protective layer of aluminum oxide (Al_2O_3), sometimes called corundum. This clear material is even stronger than the aluminum beneath it.

So in a way, you can never see pure aluminum. But in another way, you can—because it's what you see as you look through that transparent outer layer. In other words, aluminum can't rust because it has already rusted. Make sense?

WHEN WAS ALUMINUM DISCOVERED?

People have been using the words "alum" and "alumen" since ancient times to describe many different chemical compounds—although the earliest people didn't recognize them as compounds, they just considered them to be pure minerals. We now know that these compounds contained the element aluminum—sometimes in very complicated combinations.

The ancient Egyptians and Greeks used alum for dyeing clothes, for treating leather, and to stop bleeding wounds. By the 18th century, scientists were on the hunt for the basics of chemistry, breaking things up into their smallest component parts. German chemist Andreas Marggraf experimented on alum in the 1750s, eventually extracting a substance that he called alumina. This turned out to be aluminum oxide, which forms the rust-proofing outer layer around pure aluminum.

HANS CHRISTIAN OERSTED

Marggraf knew that he had discovered an oxide and not a pure element, but he was sure that it contained a new element. It took almost 60 years for another scientist, Sir Humphry Davy, to come close. He used electricity to decompose alumina and obtained a metal—but even this metal was an alloy, a mixture of more than one metallic element. Nevertheless, he called this new metal aluminum.

Aluminum was finally isolated in 1825 by Hans Christian Oersted in Copenhagen, Denmark, using a process that was time-consuming and produced very little aluminum. Oersted shared his notes with Friedrich Woehler of Germany, who improved Oersted's method and isolated larger amounts of pure aluminum in 1827.

WHERE IS ALUMINUM USED?

Ladies and gentlemen, your attention, please! You are about to be introduced to an element that can only be described as a supermetal. "A supermetal?" you say scornfully. "That's quite a claim to make. Where's the evidence?"

Ah—*evidence*. Very scientific! Well, apart from being one of the most plentiful elements on Earth (and the most abundant metal), aluminum is inexpensive, does not wear out easily, and has no odor (making it good for food packaging). It's also lightweight, strong, and a good conductor of electricity.

Convinced? Need some specific uses? OK, here goes. But remember, this is just the tip of the iceberg, and we could almost use up all of the pages in this book trying to list them all. Aluminum is the main ingredient in just about every aircraft body. Foil that's supposedly "tin" is usually made of aluminum. So are garden greenhouses. And many smartphones. And orbiting satellites. And bicycles. And rocket fuel. And frying pans. And coins... You get the picture?

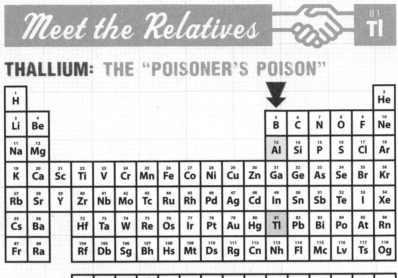
81
Tl

THALLIUM: THE "POISONER'S POISON"

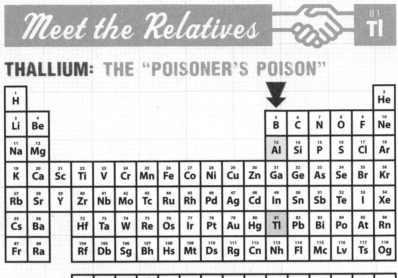

Aluminum may be mostly safe and familiar, but it has a devious cousin: thallium (Tl). It lies below aluminum in the same group of the periodic table. Like aluminum, it produces a salt when mixed with sulfuric acid (which is a compound of hydrogen, sulfur, and oxygen: H_2SO_4).

Aluminum sulfate (the result of that mixture) is used to purify water, to help colorful dyes work on textiles, and even as an ingredient in baking powder. Thallium sulfate, however, can be fatal to humans, even in doses as small as a quarter of a teaspoon mixed into water or food. Murder-mystery writers such as Agatha Christie, who was a pharmacist's assistant, knew of its devious properties and used it in many stories—making it the "poisoner's poison."

DANGER LEVEL

☢ ☢ ☢ ☢ ☢

Most sources will say that aluminum is harmless. After all, whoever got hurt touching a soda can? But very fine powdered aluminum can be really dangerous because it reacts more easily with other elements. That reactivity is why it's an ingredient in rocket fuel and modern photographic flash powder (see page 104).

FEELING A LITTLE TINNY

If you really want to know how dangerous aluminum can be, sit down and watch *The Wizard of Oz* again — in particular, check out the Tin Man. Jack Haley was the actor who played that part, singing "If I Only Had a Heart" and helping Dorothy find the Wizard. But the part originally belonged to Buddy Ebsen, a young actor and dancer.

The producers tried hard to find the best way to make Ebsen's face look "tinny," and eventually they used white face paint coated with aluminum dust. Ebsen had learned his lines and the words to all the songs, but he began to feel ill just before filming began. He got cramps and found it hard to breathe. Ebsen was rushed to the hospital, where his lungs failed briefly. Doctors identified the problem as an allergic reaction to the aluminum dust on his face, which he inhaled . . . leading to an infection of his lungs.

Family members feared for his life at one point, but he gradually began to recover. In the meantime, though, the film studio decided that "the show must go on," and Ebsen was replaced with Jack Haley. This time they took more care with the makeup, mixing it into a paste rather than exposing Haley to the aluminum dust. You can still hear Ebsen in the movie, though: It's his voice (and not Haley's) singing "We're Off to See the Wizard."

EXPERIMENT *with the* ELEMENT

Aluminum foil is great for preserving things, right? Like the drumsticks from the Thanksgiving turkey or brownies to take on a hike. It's not the sort of thing that just wastes away . . . or is it?

EXPERIMENT 13 TIME FACTOR: 1 DAY

CURSES—FOILED AGAIN!

Metals do some unusual things when they're thrown (or stuck) together. Sometimes it's hard to work out why one of the metals seems to have lost its strength. That's what happened in 1963 when metal on the USS *Thresher* submarine corroded, causing it to sink, along with its 129 crew members.

You'll have a much safer glimpse at the same process with this copper–aluminum combination. It's simple and doesn't require much equipment. Just remember to use a penny dated before 1983; that was the year that pennies stopped being made mainly of copper.

YOU WILL NEED

- **Scissors**
- **Aluminum foil**
- **Drinking glass**
- **Penny (1982 or older)**
- **Water**

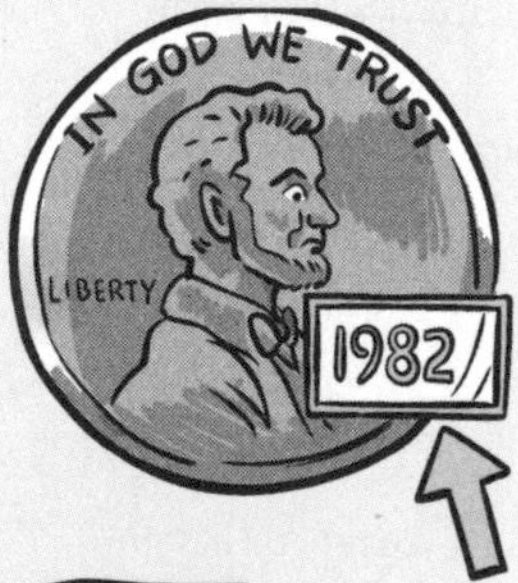

IN GOD WE TRUST
LIBERTY
1982

METHOD

1. Use the scissors to cut a piece of foil to form a roughly 2-inch (5 cm) square.

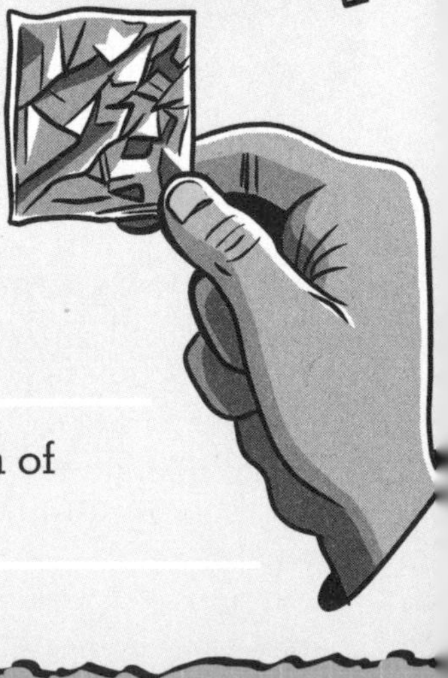

2. Put the foil square at the bottom of the glass.

3 Place the coin carefully on top of the foil.

4 Fill the glass slowly with water, taking care not to disturb the coin resting on the foil.

5 Leave the glass for 24 hours.

6 Observe it now, and note the cloudiness of the liquid (indicating that the aluminum is corroding).

7 Pour the liquid out and remove the coin and foil. You'll see that the aluminum has corroded most where it was touching the coin.

HEY, WHAT'S GOING ON?

The copper reacts with the water to create a slight electrical current, which causes the aluminum to corrode (disintegrate) slowly. The process is called galvanic corrosion, and usually involves two metals stuck together. The aluminum corrodes faster than the copper because the aluminum's ions (electrically charged atoms) are drawn away from it more readily than from the other metal. And it was galvanic corrosion that caused the *Thresher* submarine tragedy.

ATOMIC NUMBER: 14	ELECTRONS IN OUTERMOST SHELL: 4
ATOMIC WEIGHT: 28.0855	MELTING POINT: 2,577°F (1,414°C)
ELEMENT SYMBOL: Si	BOILING POINT: 5,909°F (3,265°C)

CHAPTER 12

SILICON

1 H																	2 He
3 Li	4 Be											5 B	6 C	7 N	8 O	9 F	10 Ne
11 Na	12 Mg											13 Al	14 Si	15 P	16 S	17 Cl	18 Ar
19 K	20 Ca	21 Sc	22 Ti	23 V	24 Cr	25 Mn	26 Fe	27 Co	28 Ni	29 Cu	30 Zn	31 Ga	32 Ge	33 As	34 Se	35 Br	36 Kr
37 Rb	38 Sr	39 Y	40 Zr	41 Nb	42 Mo	43 Tc	44 Ru	45 Rh	46 Pd	47 Ag	48 Cd	49 In	50 Sn	51 Sb	52 Te	53 I	54 Xe
55 Cs	56 Ba		72 Hf	73 Ta	74 W	75 Re	76 Os	77 Ir	78 Pt	79 Au	80 Hg	81 Tl	82 Pb	83 Bi	84 Po	85 At	86 Rn
87 Fr	88 Ra		104 Rf	105 Db	106 Sg	107 Bh	108 Hs	109 Mt	110 Ds	111 Rg	112 Cn	113 Nh	114 Fl	115 Mc	116 Lv	117 Ts	118 Og

57 La	58 Ce	59 Pr	60 Nd	61 Pm	62 Sm	63 Eu	64 Gd	65 Tb	66 Dy	67 Ho	68 Er	69 Tm	70 Yb	71 Lu
89 Ac	90 Th	91 Pa	92 U	93 Np	94 Pu	95 Am	96 Cm	97 Bk	98 Cf	99 Es	100 Fm	101 Md	102 No	103 Lr

A number of perhaps not-so-reliable websites have reported that senior US military officials have held secret meetings with representatives of other planets as recently as 2009. "Unnamed sources" who were present at these meetings described the aliens as wearing special suits that let them appear in different forms to the human beings. Without the suits, these aliens "were ceramic looking and were composed primarily of silicon with maybe a little carbon."

Whoa—hold up. You can't believe everything you see online, right? But there's more than a kernel of truth in the story. Some of the world's leading scientists really do believe that silicon could be the basis of life on some planets in the universe, just as carbon is on Earth. Not bad for an element that many people have associated mainly with bricks and cement for many years. But we don't need aliens to make us see this element in a new light: Every time you pick up a smartphone or send an email, you're relying on silicon, and it has already completely transformed our own world.

WHAT DOES SILICON LOOK LIKE?

Pure silicon is crystal-shaped, with shiny silver edges that are highly reflective. It is strong but brittle, and it chips easily. Although it is very rare to find pure silicon, it is the second-most-abundant element in the Earth's crust, after oxygen. That silicon is locked in compounds making up some of the most familiar types of rock, including quartz, feldspar, granite, clay, and mica.

Silicon is in the carbon group of elements, so it forms compounds in similar ways to other elements in the group. Remember, a single carbon atom combines with two oxygen atoms to form carbon dioxide (CO_2), which we know mainly as a gas that we exhale or as stuff dissolved in liquids (think of the bubbles in sodas). A single silicon atom also combines with two oxygen atoms, and the result is silicon dioxide (SiO_2)—but that compound does not dissolve in water and you can't imagine breathing it out . . . it's sand!

WHEN WAS SILICON DISCOVERED?

The name "silicon" comes from the Latin word *silicus*, meaning "flint." Flint is a form of quartz, one of the minerals that contains silicon. Considering that flint tools were made about 2.5 million years ago, you could say that silicon was "discovered" during the Stone Age.

Identifying and isolating the element silicon was a different matter. In 1789, French chemist Antoine Lavoisier suggested that the mineral quartz contained an element that had not yet been identified. Thirty-five years later, Swedish chemist Jöns Jakob Berzelius succeeded in isolating that new element. When he named it, he retained the Latin word *silicus* and added the ending "ium" so it sounded like other elements: silicium.

Scottish chemist Thomas Thomson argued that the "ium" ending made it sound like a metal when, in fact, the new element behaved more like some of its nonmetal neighbors, such as carbon and boron. The scientific community agreed with Thomson and adopted his suggested "on" ending, giving us "silicon."

WHERE IS SILICON USED?

Silicon has had a rich and varied history alongside human beings. We've moved on from flint tools, but we still use silicon (in its compound forms) for many purposes. Look through a window and you're looking through silicon—glass is made by heating up and liquefying sand, which is really silica (silicon dioxide). You might also have seen the word "silicon" on various household items, including cookware, fabric softener, and solar panels. Silicon carbide is one of the hardest substances on Earth, and it's used to produce bearings and mechanical seals that last longer than most metals.

One of the most important uses of silicon is as a semiconductor, a key feature of nearly every high-tech product that you can buy—cell phones, laptops, tablets, digital cameras . . . the list gets bigger by the day, it seems. An electrical current is simply the flow of electrons: A good conductor (a metal such as copper, for example) has free electrons that can become part of that flow, or current. An insulator (such as glass) stops such a flow.

So how does silicon come into play in all of this? Well, atoms of silicon, in a normal state, have their four outer electrons bonded with four outer electrons of other silicon atoms. This "locked tight" arrangement leads the silicon to form crystals, making it a poor conductor. When you add a small amount of another element, such as boron or phosphorus, however, it changes the

way the silicon crystals behave with electrical currents. The new element can fit into the crystal structure, but it might have five (rather than four) outer electrons. Four of those five electrons would bond with four neighboring silicon electrons, but the extra electron would be free to carry a charge. This process is called "doping," and it's really useful because it enables engineers to turn silicon into a conductor, an insulator, or something that allows electrical current in one direction only. The term for this "not quite a real conductor" is "semiconductor," and semiconductors form the backbone of modern electrical equipment.

GROUP 14: ROOM FOR MORE LIFE?

1 H																	2 He
3 Li	4 Be											5 B	6 C	7 N	8 O	9 F	10 Ne
11 Na	12 Mg											13 Al	14 Si	15 P	16 S	17 Cl	18 Ar
19 K	20 Ca	21 Sc	22 Ti	23 V	24 Cr	25 Mn	26 Fe	27 Co	28 Ni	29 Cu	30 Zn	31 Ga	32 Ge	33 As	34 Se	35 Br	36 Kr
37 Rb	38 Sr	39 Y	40 Zr	41 Nb	42 Mo	43 Tc	44 Ru	45 Rh	46 Pd	47 Ag	48 Cd	49 In	50 Sn	51 Sb	52 Te	53 I	54 Xe
55 Cs	56 Ba		72 Hf	73 Ta	74 W	75 Re	76 Os	77 Ir	78 Pt	79 Au	80 Hg	81 Tl	82 Pb	83 Bi	84 Po	85 At	86 Rn
87 Fr	88 Ra		104 Rf	105 Db	106 Sg	107 Bh	108 Hs	109 Mt	110 Ds	111 Rg	112 Cn	113 Nh	114 Fl	115 Mc	116 Lv	117 Ts	118 Og

57 La	58 Ce	59 Pr	60 Nd	61 Pm	62 Sm	63 Eu	64 Gd	65 Tb	66 Dy	67 Ho	68 Er	69 Tm	70 Yb	71 Lu
89 Ac	90 Th	91 Pa	92 U	93 Np	94 Pu	95 Am	96 Cm	97 Bk	98 Cf	99 Es	100 Fm	101 Md	102 No	103 Lr

What makes scientists and science-fiction authors consider silicon as a possible model of extraterrestrial life? Well, it's mostly because of where it sits on the periodic table. Group 14 is known as the carbon group, named after the element that lies directly above silicon. Carbon lies at the heart of life as we know it. It can form complicated compounds thanks to its four outer-shell (valence) electrons—meaning that a single carbon atom can combine with four other atoms all at the same time. Pretty impressive!

So far, so good. Now silicon, being part of the same group, also has four valence electrons. Like carbon, it can bond with up to four other atoms, so it can also form complex molecules. Plus, silicon isn't just locked in the

Earth's crust: It's the eighth-most-common element in the universe.

Anything wrong with this "silicon life" idea? Well, silicon can form big, complex molecules, but those molecules are considered "boring" compared to those formed by carbon. Silicon doesn't bond with as many different elements as carbon does, and that lack of variety makes it hard to imagine that silicon molecules could carry out the huge range of tasks that carbon molecules do—important stuff like growth, development, reproduction, and so on.

Another big advantage for carbon is that it dissolves in water, in the form of carbon dioxide (CO_2). With this waterborne carbon dissolved all across Earth's largest habitat (the oceans), carbon-based life had an enormous "breeding ground." Silicon's equivalent compound, silicon dioxide (SiO_2), does not dissolve in water.

DANGER LEVEL

☢ ☢ ☢ ☢ ☢

Pure silicon has no known harmful effects, but the fine powder of some of its compounds can cause respiratory problems after they have been inhaled over time. Six of these compounds, known as asbestos, were once common building materials. Now they are banned in most countries because they have been linked to deadly cancers.

EXPERIMENT with the ELEMENT

Silicon can't make up its mind whether it's attracted to water (hydrophilic) or repelled by it (hydrophobic). When it's in a compound with oxygen as silicon dioxide (also known as silica, or sand), it does attract water. On its own, it usually repels it. The first experiment shows how sand can be turned into a "water hater" by treating it with a hydrophobic compound. You'll be making magic sand. The second harnesses the hydrophilic, water-attracting properties of silica to dry flowers quickly.

DON'T SAND SO CLOSE TO ME

Magic sand was first used to deal with dangerous oil spills. The sand would attach itself to oil and then sink (because it wouldn't be attracted to the water), allowing the oil–sand mixture to be collected below the water's surface. Unfortunately, it is too expensive to deal with oil spills in this way, so most people know of magic sand as a fun substance to use to build underwater sand castles.

Make some of your own, and you'll find that it's a great way to see silicon in action.

YOU WILL NEED

- ◆ **Aluminum foil**
- ◆ **Baking pan**
- ◆ **2 pounds (0.9 kg) of sand**
  (you can buy sand at home improvement or pet stores if you're not near a beach or lake)
- ◆ **An adult to help**
- ◆ **Fabric protector spray**
  (such as ScotchGard Protector)
- ◆ **Popsicle stick**
- ◆ **2 spoons**
- ◆ **Drinking glass**
- ◆ **Water**
- ◆ **Cooking oil**

METHOD

1. Spread a sheet of foil to cover the baking pan, wrapping it tightly over each edge.

2. Pour enough sand into the pan to make a layer about ¼ to ½ inch (6 to 12 mm) thick. Shake the pan a little to spread the sand around evenly.

3. Have an adult spray the sand evenly with ScotchGard so that the layer is completely covered. Let it dry for a few minutes.

FABRIC PROTECTOR SPRAY

4 Rough up the sand with the Popsicle stick to expose sand that hasn't been sprayed.

5 Repeat Steps 3 and 4 about four or five more times to make sure that all of the sand has a good coating of ScotchGard.

COOKING OIL

6 Let the sand dry for about three hours, preferably in a still, sunny area.

7 The magic sand is now complete. Try taking a tablespoon of it and sprinkling it into a glass of water. You'll see how it would help drag oil from the surface of a spill.

8 Gently pour a tablespoon of oil onto the water's surface and sprinkle another tablespoon of magic sand onto it—did you clear the oil slick?

HEY, WHAT'S GOING ON?

The ScotchGard contains compounds such as perfluoro-butanesulfonic acid—pray that you never get that word in a spelling bee—that strengthen the hydrophobic properties of the sand (which is mainly silicon dioxide). It's all down to how "polar" (like magnetic fields) the compounds are, including water. And since hydrophobic means "repelled by water," the grains of sand behave a little like people who've heard something creepy in a haunted house—they draw closer to each other for protection. The grains of sand draw into one another to reduce surface area when they're exposed to water. They form cylinders as a result.

FAST-TRACK FOSSILS

Silica gel comes in small packets with all sorts of products that need to be kept dry—cameras, shoes, electrical goods, and many more. You've probably seen those packets with "Do not eat" written on them. (That's right, don't even think about it!) In this experiment you'll use a couple of silica gel packets to dry some flowers so fast that it will seem like time-lapse photography or fossils in the making.

YOU WILL NEED

- ◆ **1 or 2 packets of silica gel**
- ◆ **Aluminum foil**
- ◆ **Baking tray**
- ◆ **Small plastic food container with airtight lid**
- ◆ **Flower petals (any type, as long as they can fit inside the container easily)**

WARNING! Have an adult supervise any baking.

METHOD

1 Pour the silica gel onto a piece of foil.

2 Check for the color. If it's blue, go on to Step 7. If it's pink, continue.

3 Heat an oven to 250°F (120°C).

4 Place the foil (with the gel) on the baking tray.

5 When the oven is warm, add the tray and bake it for two hours.

6 Take the tray from the oven and let it cool for 15 minutes.

7 Pour the silica gel into the bottom of the food container and shake it gently to spread the gel evenly.

8 Lay the petals carefully on the gel.

9 Seal the container and leave it overnight.

10 Observe how the removal of the water has affected the flowers—do they look like fossils?

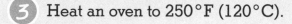

HEY, WHAT'S GOING ON?

The hydrophilic gel attracts moisture from the air around it and from other objects, such as the flower petals. You'll see what effect the water has on the appearance of the petals—especially after their overnight session. Silica gel turns pink when it has absorbed water. It can't be used when it's that color, but can be revived by being heated in the oven. Then it returns to its normal blue color.

ATOMIC NUMBER: 15	ELECTRONS IN OUTERMOST SHELL: 5
ATOMIC WEIGHT: 30.9738	MELTING POINT: 111.47°F (44.15°C)
ELEMENT SYMBOL: P	BOILING POINT: 808°F (431°C)

CHAPTER 13

PHOSPHORUS

1 H																	2 He
3 Li	4 Be											5 B	6 C	7 N	8 O	9 F	10 Ne
11 Na	12 Mg											13 Al	14 Si	15 P	16 S	17 Cl	18 Ar
19 K	20 Ca	21 Sc	22 Ti	23 V	24 Cr	25 Mn	26 Fe	27 Co	28 Ni	29 Cu	30 Zn	31 Ga	32 Ge	33 As	34 Se	35 Br	36 Kr
37 Rb	38 Sr	39 Y	40 Zr	41 Nb	42 Mo	43 Tc	44 Ru	45 Rh	46 Pd	47 Ag	48 Cd	49 In	50 Sn	51 Sb	52 Te	53 I	54 Xe
55 Cs	56 Ba		72 Hf	73 Ta	74 W	75 Re	76 Os	77 Ir	78 Pt	79 Au	80 Hg	81 Tl	82 Pb	83 Bi	84 Po	85 At	86 Rn
87 Fr	88 Ra		104 Rf	105 Db	106 Sg	107 Bh	108 Hs	109 Mt	110 Ds	111 Rg	112 Cn	113 Nh	114 Fl	115 Mc	116 Lv	117 Ts	118 Og

	57 La	58 Ce	59 Pr	60 Nd	61 Pm	62 Sm	63 Eu	64 Gd	65 Tb	66 Dy	67 Ho	68 Er	69 Tm	70 Yb	71 Lu
	89 Ac	90 Th	91 Pa	92 U	93 Np	94 Pu	95 Am	96 Cm	97 Bk	98 Cf	99 Es	100 Fm	101 Md	102 No	103 Lr

By now you should know that very few of our dozens and dozens of elements are around us in their pure form. Ancient people, of course, discovered gold and silver, but what about hydrogen? Or carbon? Or oxygen? Nope—finding all of those involved scientific exploration, because those elements were mixed up with others in compounds.

So which was the first element to be discovered through that sort of exploration? The answer is . . . drumroll, please . . . phosphorus! What's more, its discoverer, Hennig Brand, wasn't looking to find a missing piece in the periodic table. He was looking for something far more attractive: the secret to eternal life. Well, needless to say, that didn't exactly work out. The element that he isolated is certainly necessary for life, but it can also cause dramatic death.

WHAT DOES PHOSPHORUS LOOK LIKE?

Phosphorus is an element that can exist in different forms, called allotropes, depending on how its atoms are bonded together. The different allotropes of phosphorus are known by their color, although if you looked closely, you would see that the real difference is in the pattern of the bonds between the phosphorus atoms. The most common is white phosphorus—it's also the least stable, least dense, and most reactive of them. It is a white-yellow waxy solid. White phosphorus glows in the dark when it is exposed to pure oxygen, and it ignites when it comes into contact with air.

If you need an example of how different these forms can be, consider some of the allotropes of carbon: Soft graphite and hard diamond are both made of pure carbon, although they are tied together with different bonds. They are two allotropes of carbon. Graphite is made of layers of carbon atoms. The atoms on each layer are bound to each other, but there's little bond between the

ALL ABOUT ALLOTROPES

The atoms of many elements join up (bond) with themselves to make larger molecules. They don't always join up in the same way, though, and because of that, these different forms—called allotropes—can look or behave differently.

Exposure to light and heat causes white phosphorus to change into red phosphorus. In fact, it would be hard to see pure white phosphorus, because if you could, it would already be changing into the red variety. That's why even "white" phosphorus looks a little yellow—it's beginning to change color.

layers. That makes graphite slippery and easy to break. A diamond, on the other hand, is a tight "ball" of carbon atoms. They are bound to other carbon atoms from every direction, making diamond very hard to pull apart.

WHEN WAS PHOSPHORUS DISCOVERED?

During the Middle Ages, before the modern sciences of chemistry, biology, and physics developed as serious studies, most experiments were carried out by alchemists. These secretive "scientists" believed that matter contained almost magical powers. Some of them spent their lives trying to turn "base metals" such as lead or iron into valuable gold. Others set their sights even higher, trying to find the secret of eternal youth.

Alchemists believed that a magical substance, called the philosopher's stone, could achieve their aims. (You might know this term already—the original British title for the first Harry Potter novel is *Harry Potter and*

HENNIG BRAND

the Philosopher's Stone.) A German alchemist named Hennig Brand isolated and identified the element phosphorus in 1669. Unlike modern scientists, who announce their discoveries for all to learn from, Brand kept quiet and sold the formula to other alchemists. The news of the element slipped out only gradually.

WHERE IS PHOSPHORUS USED?

Red phosphorus is the most common form of the element, and it is the only phosphorus that you'll ever come across—unless you're really unlucky. It does ignite easily, but only after it has been warmed by friction. That's why it is used in matches. The more flammable form, white phosphorus, is highly dangerous and has been used in many horrible weapons because of its ability to burn quickly and unstoppably.

Phosphorus is also used to help produce steel and bronze, but perhaps the most beneficial use of phosphorus comes from the compounds it forms with oxygen. Every form of life that we know depends on these compounds, known as phosphates, to survive. It is a vital ingredient in DNA, the "biological blueprint of life," and the energy-storing chemical compound ATP. Many plant fertilizers also contain phosphates.

In fact, sometimes you have to remind yourself that this is the same element that's essential for our well-being and plays a central part in the DNA compound (which carries the instructions for our growth and development). The dangers associated with phosphorus are linked to its glowing, burning qualities. Pure phosphorus can burn underwater—or inside anyone who happens to swallow it.

Phosphorus is also an important ingredient in the deadly poison sarin, which stops the nervous system from sending messages—such as telling muscles to make you breathe. The United Nations considers sarin to be a weapon of mass destruction, and it was detected in some of the victims of the bloody civil war in Syria.

Meet the Relatives 🤝 51 Sb

ANTIMONY: NEFERTITI'S MASCARA?

The element antimony (Sb) is two places down from phosphorus in group 15 of the periodic table. It is a semimetal that nowadays is used to harden other metals and to make flameproof paints and ceramics. The name "antimony" comes from two Greek words meaning "not alone," which makes sense, because the element is normally found in compounds. The ancient Egyptians used one of those compounds, stibnite (made of antimony and sulfur), as a black powder for eye makeup. Known as kohl, this powder gave Egyptian women the distinctive look that we associate with Nefertiti and other queens. The Egyptians believed this look was a sign of holiness and would help the person in the afterlife journey.

SHERLOCK HOLMES AND THE DEVIL'S ELEMENT

Phosphorus has sometimes been called "the devil's element," perhaps because of its link with the dark art of alchemy. It doesn't help matters to mention that phosphorus often appears in a ghostly glow. Sherlock Holmes concluded that the legendary "hound of the Baskervilles" (a fierce, ghostly dog that seemed to glow) was really a normal dog whose snout had been painted with "a cunning preparation of phosphorus." (Even Holmes could get things wrong: Phosphorus would have killed the dog!) But even if you disregard superstition and detective novels, you can find lots of reasons to be careful with this element.

DANGER LEVEL

The real danger, of course, comes from white phosphorus. Luckily, this element is usually locked into compounds that offset its destructive properties. And those properties are pretty extreme, producing poisonous fumes or producing dramatic explosions when it mixes with lots of other elements and compounds.

EXPERIMENT *with the* ELEMENT

Up to now, all of the experiments have been suggested as a way to improve your own knowledge about an element or elements in general. This phosphorus experiment helps you do just that, plus you'll have a chance to do a *really* huge favor for anyone who has a cat. You might need to hold your nose a little at first, though.

PLAYING CAT DETECTIVE

Sherlock Holmes had his science a bit mixed up when he proposed that phosphorus was the solution to the *Hound of the Baskervilles* mystery. Now's your chance to outdo the supersleuth with your own knowledge of phosphorus. And it won't be with a scary hound, but with the family cat. The living room's stinky, and you know that kitty must have squirted somewhere—but where? That's where you come in as the scientific detective.

Three basic facts will help you get started. The first is that cat's urine has a high concentration of phosphorus. The second is that phosphorus shows up as a glow when ultraviolent light shines on it. (Just as there are sounds we can't hear, we can't see ultraviolet light because it's outside our range of vision—that's why it's also called a "black light.") The third fact is that you can get "black light" bulbs easily. So, replace one of the light bulbs in the smelly room with the black light bulb and start hunting. And if your cat is, shall we say, "well-behaved," you could still do this experiment in the room with the litter tray.

YOU WILL NEED

- **Room affected by "cat smell" (or a room with a litter tray)**
- **Black light bulb**

WARNING! Make sure an adult supervises the change of bulbs.

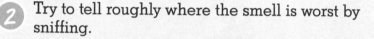

1. Decide on the room where you will be the detective. (If there's a real problem, just follow your nose.)

2. Try to tell roughly where the smell is worst by sniffing.

3. Replace a normal light bulb with a black light bulb in the nearest lamp.

4. Turn off any other lights. (Close the curtains if it's daytime.)

5. Look around for traces of glowing light. A new stain will appear bright yellow; older stains will be dull yellow or green.

HEY, WHAT'S GOING ON?

Exposure to ultraviolet light causes some of the phosphorus electrons to absorb energy and become "excited," jumping to an energy level (or "shell") that's farther from the nucleus. The neon electrons did just that in the earlier experiment (see page 84). And like those neon electrons, they discharge light as they return to their normal state.

ATOMIC NUMBER: 16	ELECTRONS IN OUTERMOST SHELL: 6
ATOMIC WEIGHT: 32.065	MELTING POINT: 203.5°F (95.3°C)
ELEMENT SYMBOL: S	BOILING POINT: 832.3°F (444.6°C)

CHAPTER 14

SULFUR

Well, there's one thing that you can say about sulfur: It certainly has a history. Foul-smelling, smoking, burning, and destructive, it created an atmosphere all its own—a scary, evil atmosphere. It crops up regularly in the Bible, usually when people are receiving a terrible punishment—and always with the old-fashioned word for sulfur, "brimstone." In the Old Testament, the sinful cities of Sodom and Gomorrah were destroyed with a rain of fire and brimstone.

OK, so things don't look good for sulfur's reputation. Then there's the matter of the smell . . . pee-ew! But like so many elements, sulfur is able to spring some surprises. You might see it in a new light. In the meantime, hold your nose and read on.

WHAT DOES SULFUR LOOK LIKE?

Pure sulfur is a pale yellow, soft, odorless solid, and it reacts with most elements to create stable compounds. Sulfur remains solid in water and burns (creating sulfur dioxide) with a blue flame. Maybe this section should be called "What does sulfur smell like?" though, since that's how most people first come across it. It's linked to an all-star cast of the nastiest, grossest, rottenest smells—eggs gone bad, garlic, skunk odor . . . and the end result of eating too many baked beans.

Sulfur's defenders might point out that these smells don't necessarily come from pure sulfur. They're really the result of sulfur forming compounds with other elements. It could be a sulfur atom combining with two oxygen atoms to create sulfur dioxide (SO_2), usually when sulfur is burned. That gas is smelly, but if sulfur combines with water in the atmosphere it can create an acid that eats away at rocks when it falls as rain (that's what we call "acid rain").

WHEN WAS SULFUR DISCOVERED?

Sulfur is another element that ancient people identified. We can learn some of its history by looking at its names. One possible root of our modern word "sulfur" is the Arabic word *sufra*, which means "yellow." That's a good description of the color of pure sulfur. Or take the old-fashioned English word "brimstone"—the one that crops up so often in the Bible. That meant "burning stone," another good description of the pure element.

Where did those ancient people find all that pure sulfur? You don't normally find sulfur just lying around. But you *do* find it in areas of volcanic activity, such as Mount Vesuvius near Pompeii and Mount Etna on the Italian island of Sicily (both of which were well known to ancient people). Pure sulfur burns around the steaming mouths of these volcanoes, creating a scary glow and giving off a strong smell.

Our scientific—as opposed to religious or mythical— understanding of sulfur dates from the scientific and industrial revolutions during the 18th century, when new discoveries powered an age of invention. And it was one of the great scientists of that period, Antoine Lavoisier of France, who identified sulfur as an element in 1777.

This same atmosphere of discovery and invention led to new ways of using and extracting sulfur. No one felt like building sulfur mines near the peaks of active volcanoes—can you blame them?—so people looked for new ways of extracting sulfur from compounds. By far the most successful way of obtaining sulfur came through the Frasch process.

FRASCH PROCESS

In 1894, Herman Frasch, a German American chemist, demonstrated a method of extracting sulfur that would otherwise be trapped beneath layers of other rocks. Holes were drilled through outer (nonsulfur) layers. Water, heated under pressure to a temperature above the melting point of sulfur, was then pumped in pipes through a hole. This caused the sulfur to melt, and it was then pumped back out to the surface through another pipe.

WHERE IS SULFUR USED?

Considering its explosive power and "hellish" reputation—not to mention that smell—sulfur comes in pretty handy. It's mainly used to make sulfuric acid (combined with hydrogen and oxygen). This acid is used to make fertilizer, automobile batteries, paper, detergents, paints, and many other industrial and agricultural products.

Pure sulfur is also important. Our bodies need it to build proteins and other vital molecules. It is useful as a treatment against acne and athlete's foot because it destroys bacteria and treats fungal infection. Pure sulfur is also an important dehydrating (water-removing) substance, helping us preserve dried fruit such as raisins and currants. It's also used in sugar refining, mineral extraction, and purifying water supplies.

Meet the Relatives — 18 Ar

ARGON: WHAT ABOUT ME?

As you've seen, sulfur's row (period) is full of explosive, reactive elements. So it's no surprise that sulfur's next-door neighbor and the star of the next chapter, chlorine (Cl), keeps that scary theme going. But what about argon (Ar) over there at the right, at the end of the line? Well, no offense, but there's not a whole lot to say. Why not? Well, nothing against argon, but its story is pretty similar to that of helium (see page 11) and neon (see page 77). That's because its group (the vertical column) defines it as a noble gas—and it's hard to get any reaction from it.

A DEADLY INGREDIENT

Humankind's first impressions of sulfur—steaming and bubbling and burning at the mouth of volcanoes—obviously got people thinking of using it as a weapon. In 515 CE, the Byzantines (inheritors of the Eastern Roman Empire) used a flaming substance called "Greek fire" to defeat opponents in a naval battle. It's likely that it was made primarily with sulfur.

A more lasting contribution came from China about 400 years later. Alchemists (remember those guys?) came up with something that would provide instant destruction: gunpowder. The key ingredient? Yep, sulfur.

DANGER LEVEL

Pure sulfur is pretty harmless, but you need to be careful if you're anywhere near some of the compounds that sulfur forms, such as carbon disulfide, hydrogen sulfide, and sulfur dioxide. Depending on how strong they are—and that strength is usually measured in parts per million (how many parts of the substance are mixed in with a million parts of air)—these compounds range from mildly irritating to deadly. Exposure to just 20 parts per million (ppm) of hydrogen sulfide can permanently damage your eyes, and a concentration of 700 ppm is deadly.

EXPERIMENT with the ELEMENT

Enough of that fire and brimstone. Here's an experiment to restore sulfur's reputation. OK, it's not the sulfur that's saving the day so much as your understanding of it. You're going to be working with another element, silver, and restoring it to its former glory.

SAVE THAT SILVER!

If you've ever wondered why people seem to love polishing all the silver in the house, it's because those brilliant silver knives, forks, and spoons have a habit of losing their shine over time. The process is called tarnishing, and it's actually a chemical reaction.

The silver reacts with sulfur that's in the air, coating it with a dull compound called silver sulfide (the "sulfide" is a clue). When you polish, you're removing the silver sulfide from the surface of the silver to reveal the shiny metal underneath. But removing silver sulfide means removing some of the silver itself (which is part of the compound). What if you could reverse the chemical reaction so the sulfur would be removed from the compound and the silver would be back just as it was?

That's what this experiment sets out to do. But first, ask permission from your parents and get them to choose which tarnished silver you can use. If your "silverware" isn't made of real silver, ask Mom or Dad if they have any silver jewelry instead. Still no silver? No problem—you can also do the experiment with tarnished pennies (which are coated with copper sulfide).

WARNING! Make sure you have an adult with you at all times to be in charge of boiling and pouring the water.

- Saucepan wide enough to hold several pieces of silver laid out flat
- Aluminum foil
- Several pieces of tarnished silver (such as forks or spoons) or several tarnished pennies
- Adult, to boil the water
- Measuring pitcher
- 8 cups (1.9 l) of water
- Second saucepan big enough to hold at least 2 quarts for boiling water
- Kitchen mitts
- Sink
- Cup measure
- ½ cup (120 ml) of baking soda

METHOD

 Line the bottom of the first saucepan with aluminum foil.

 Lay the tarnished silver at the bottom of the saucepan so that the pieces touch the foil.

3 Measure out 8 cups of water, pour it into the second saucepan, and bring it to a boil on a stove.

4 Take the saucepan with boiling water and place it carefully in the sink.

5 Add the baking soda to the boiling water and let the mixture froth up.

6 Pour this mixture into the first pan, completely covering the silver.

7 Within a minute or two, most of the tarnish should be gone, and the silver will be shinier.

HEY, WHAT'S GOING ON?

Remember that the tarnish was actually a coating of silver sulfide (or copper sulfide with the pennies). Well, it turns out that sulfur is attracted to aluminum even more than it is to silver or copper. In this reaction, sulfur atoms broke away from the silver or copper atoms and moved to attach themselves to the aluminum (which then got a layer of aluminum sulfide).

This is an example of an electrochemical reaction, because there was a small flow of electrons from the silver to the aluminum. That's why the silver had to touch the aluminum. The warm water and the baking soda acted as catalysts, ingredients that aren't part of the main chemical reaction but speed it along. Most chemical reactions take place more quickly if they are warmer. The baking soda helps remove a layer of another compound (aluminum hydroxide) from the foil so that the purer aluminum can receive the electrons more effectively.

ATOMIC NUMBER: 17	ELECTRONS IN OUTERMOST SHELL: 7
ATOMIC WEIGHT: 35.453	MELTING POINT: -150.7°F (-105.5°C)
ELEMENT SYMBOL: Cl	BOILING POINT: -29.27°F (-34.04°C)

CHAPTER 15

CHLORINE

1 H																	2 He
3 Li	4 Be											5 B	6 C	7 N	8 O	9 F	10 Ne
11 Na	12 Mg											13 Al	14 Si	15 P	16 S	17 Cl	18 Ar
19 K	20 Ca	21 Sc	22 Ti	23 V	24 Cr	25 Mn	26 Fe	27 Co	28 Ni	29 Cu	30 Zn	31 Ga	32 Ge	33 As	34 Se	35 Br	36 Kr
37 Rb	38 Sr	39 Y	40 Zr	41 Nb	42 Mo	43 Tc	44 Ru	45 Rh	46 Pd	47 Ag	48 Cd	49 In	50 Sn	51 Sb	52 Te	53 I	54 Xe
55 Cs	56 Ba		72 Hf	73 Ta	74 W	75 Re	76 Os	77 Ir	78 Pt	79 Au	80 Hg	81 Tl	82 Pb	83 Bi	84 Po	85 At	86 Rn
87 Fr	88 Ra		104 Rf	105 Db	106 Sg	107 Bh	108 Hs	109 Mt	110 Ds	111 Rg	112 Cn	113 Nh	114 Fl	115 Mc	116 Lv	117 Ts	118 Og

	57 La	58 Ce	59 Pr	60 Nd	61 Pm	62 Sm	63 Eu	64 Gd	65 Tb	66 Dy	67 Ho	68 Er	69 Tm	70 Yb	71 Lu
	89 Ac	90 Th	91 Pa	92 U	93 Np	94 Pu	95 Am	96 Cm	97 Bk	98 Cf	99 Es	100 Fm	101 Md	102 No	103 Lr

I f sulfur is an element that took us back into our past—to Biblical times and beyond—then chlorine takes us into the modern age. But not necessarily in a good way. On April 22, 1915, on a World War I battlefield in Belgium, the world saw the first effective use of a "weapon of mass destruction." The instrument of death was chlorine gas. It burns its way into someone's lungs, where it stops the person from getting air.

Luckily, science has also found ways of harnessing that same element so that it is now considered to be a lifesaver in many parts of the world. Millions of people depend on water that has been disinfected with chlorine, making the water safe to drink. And chlorine is present in about 85 percent of medicines, helping to treat conditions ranging from heart disease and arthritis to the common cold.

WHAT DOES CHLORINE LOOK LIKE?

Chlorine in its pure form is greenish-yellow, and its name even comes from the Greek word to describe that color—*chloros*. Chlorine is a dense gas with a distinctive smell. If you've ever smelled bleach (which is made with chlorine), you'll have an idea of that odor. The real thing would smell so strong that it would seem to burn its way into your head, which made it devastating as a weapon.

Luckily, you'll never come across pure chlorine in nature. Take a look at its position on the periodic table, and you should be able to work out why. There it is, in group 17, way to the right of the third period. Just one group more and you hit the noble gases . . . which means, of course, that chlorine is just one electron short of filling its outer layer with eight. So just like fluorine (see page 67), it's always teaming up with other elements to nab that single electron. Just think of one of its best-known compounds, sodium chloride (table salt). Sodium has one spare electron and chlorine needs one: Now *there's* a match made in heaven—or in the world of chemistry.

WHEN WAS CHLORINE DISCOVERED?

Chlorine is one of the elements with a definite "year of discovery" and discoverer. Considering how often the element hides itself in compounds—and how deadly it would be if you somehow did come across the pure form accidentally—that's not surprising. In 1774, Carl Wilhelm Scheele of Sweden was experimenting with a sample of the mineral pyrolusite. He was sure that it contained an element that hadn't yet been identified. (He was right—and he was on course to discover the element manganese, which combines with oxygen to create pyrolusite.) Scheele mixed the mineral with a strong liquid that alchemists called *spiritus salis* (which we now call hydrochloric acid). Sure enough, the mixture did produce something quite unknown—although it wasn't emerging from the pyrolusite.

The acid had broken down into its two ingredients—hydrogen and something else. He noted "a very perceptible suffocating smell, which was most oppressive to the lungs . . . and gives the water a slightly acidic taste . . . the air in it acquires a yellow color." Yep, sure sounds like chlorine! Although Scheele had produced the first pure chlorine, he wasn't sure that it was an element. Other scientists also felt that this new gas must be a compound, perhaps with oxygen. Antoine Lavoisier, "the father of modern Chemistry," did not include chlorine in his famous list of elements in 1789. It was only in 1810 that British scientist Sir Humphry Davy (busy as ever) stated that this gas was an element. And he named it chlorine.

WHERE IS CHLORINE USED?

Luckily, chlorine has gone a long way toward rebuilding its reputation as a killer. In fact, in another way, its deadliness actually saves lives. Chlorine is added to drinking water to kill disease-causing fungi and bacteria. Used in reservoirs, it can control or even eliminate mold and

slime. These measures alone would classify chlorine as a lifesaver. You've probably noticed that distinctive chlorine smell at a local swimming pool: It's an important disinfectant.

Chlorine is also used in laundry products and household disinfectants and for making textiles, petroleum products, artificial rubber, paints, and dozens of other products. But most scientists agree that its role as a disinfectant has earned chlorine's place in the Public Health Hall of Fame. Some scientists even claim that chlorine has saved more lives worldwide than any other chemical—and that includes penicillin (the stuff in antibiotic medicine).

Meet the Relatives

35
Br

BROMINE: FIT FOR A KING?

1 H												5 B	6 C	7 N	8 O	9 F	2 He
3 Li	4 Be											5 B	6 C	7 N	8 O	9 F	10 Ne
11 Na	12 Mg											13 Al	14 Si	15 P	16 S	17 Cl	18 Ar
19 K	20 Ca	21 Sc	22 Ti	23 V	24 Cr	25 Mn	26 Fe	27 Co	28 Ni	29 Cu	30 Zn	31 Ga	32 Ge	33 As	34 Se	35 Br	36 Kr
37 Rb	38 Sr	39 Y	40 Zr	41 Nb	42 Mo	43 Tc	44 Ru	45 Rh	46 Pd	47 Ag	48 Cd	49 In	50 Sn	51 Sb	52 Te	53 I	54 Xe
55 Cs	56 Ba		72 Hf	73 Ta	74 W	75 Re	76 Os	77 Ir	78 Pt	79 Au	80 Hg	81 Tl	82 Pb	83 Bi	84 Po	85 At	86 Rn
87 Fr	88 Ra		104 Rf	105 Db	106 Sg	107 Bh	108 Hs	109 Mt	110 Ds	111 Rg	112 Cn	113 Nh	114 Fl	115 Mc	116 Lv	117 Ts	118 Og

	57 La	58 Ce	59 Pr	60 Nd	61 Pm	62 Sm	63 Eu	64 Gd	65 Tb	66 Dy	67 Ho	68 Er	69 Tm	70 Yb	71 Lu
	89 Ac	90 Th	91 Pa	92 U	93 Np	94 Pu	95 Am	96 Cm	97 Bk	98 Cf	99 Es	100 Fm	101 Md	102 No	103 Lr

The next element down from chlorine in the periodic table—another member of the halogen group—is bromine (Br). You'll be able to predict, then, that it shares some characteristics with chlorine:

- Reacts easily with other elements? Yep.

- Poisonous to humans? Yes, but not as bad as chlorine.

- Useful as a bleach and disinfectant? You bet.

- A gas at room temperature? It's a liquid, but it emits strong-smelling vapors (the name "bromine" comes from the Greek word meaning "stench").

Bromine is found in seawater, so aquatic plants and animals also contain it. In ancient times, people extracted a purple coloring from the bromine-rich mucus (*gross!*) of mussels in the Mediterranean Sea. It was an expensive process, so only the richest people—such as kings—could afford this dye, known as Tyrian or royal purple.

DANGER LEVEL

Those grisly World War I experiences spelled out the dangers of chlorine in an unforgettable way. With the passage of time, people have had less and less contact with the deadly results of contact with chlorine. Instead, we think of it as something that might give a little smell to our drinking water or a stronger smell in the bathroom or at the pool. But the dangers remain very real.

EXPERIMENT *with the* ELEMENT

Here's a chance to team chlorine up with an element that you've already read about: sodium. The result is one of the most common and familiar compounds that you'll ever find—table salt, or sodium chloride.

"I'LL HAVE AN EGG FLOAT"

It's time to slip into your magician's outfit, because this experiment really works well as a trick. And like so many of the best magic tricks, the secret is very simple—the magician's skill lies in making it all look mysterious.

You're going to add salt to some warm water, and an egg will rise up. Simple as that. But there's no point mentioning this as you perform the experiment. Your audience will believe that you've added "magic crystals" to the water to make the egg float. Don't spill the beans until you've had a round of applause at the end. Oh, and don't forget to explain the chemistry.

YOU WILL NEED

- ◆ Salt
- ◆ Cup or bowl (large enough to hold 1 cup or 250 ml of salt)
- ◆ Uncooked egg
- ◆ Clear pitcher (about 1 quart)
- ◆ Warm water
- ◆ Tablespoon
- ◆ Wooden mixing spoon

METHOD

1. Add about a cupful of salt to the cup or bowl and set aside.

2. Carefully put the egg in the bottom of the pitcher.

3 Run warm water from the faucet into the pitcher until it's just over half full. You can do this in front of your audience, so they'll know it's normal water.

4 Hold the pitcher up so everyone can see that the egg is at the bottom.

5 Now tell your audience that you will add magic crystals to the water to make the egg float.

6 Add about three tablespoons of salt to the water and stir with the wooden spoon.

7 The egg might float with that much salt. If not, try two more spoonfuls, or enough until the egg rises to the top and floats.

HEY, WHAT'S GOING ON?

This experiment is all about density. Water molecules aren't very dense, which means that there's space all around them. The egg is denser than the water, so it sinks. But those spaces between the water molecules allow other substances to be mixed in. The molecules of the "magic crystals" (salt) can easily slip in between as they dissolve in the water. Why? Because salt (sodium chloride) is a compound of sodium and . . . our friend chlorine. The sodium and chlorine molecules are broken down into ions that are attracted to the hydrogen and oxygen molecules (which make up water).

These new arrivals fit right in—literally—to the water because of that attraction. The volume of the water doesn't increase, so the water mixture becomes denser. Eventually it becomes denser than the egg . . . which begins to float!

ATOMIC NUMBER: 20	ELECTRONS IN OUTERMOST SHELL: 2
ATOMIC WEIGHT: 40.078	MELTING POINT: 1,548°F (842°C)
ELEMENT SYMBOL: Ca	BOILING POINT: 2,703°F (1,484°C)

CHAPTER 16

CALCIUM

"Brush your teeth!"

"Come on, finish that glass of milk to keep your bones strong!"

"Foul ball!"

"Chalk that up to experience!"

"We who are about to die salute you!"

What links those five sentences? Give up? (Psst! Here's a hint: Read the chapter title.) OK, maybe you could have made the connection with just the first two. You've probably learned that healthy teeth and bones depend on calcium (which is contained in milk). But calcium plays a part in many other areas of our daily lives and history too.

The white stuff that marks foul lines on a baseball diamond is a calcium compound (calcium carbonate). In slightly harder form, that same compound is chalk. The last clue is a little trickier. It's what historians believe gladiators said to the Roman emperor as they entered the Colosseum to do battle. And several calcium compounds figured in the ingredients list for building that very famous arena.

Here's an element that seems to cover everything from life to death, with lots in between. It's definitely worth exploring.

WHAT DOES CALCIUM LOOK LIKE?

Well, here's what pure calcium *doesn't* look like: gleaming white like a Halloween skeleton, or freshly brushed teeth, or chalk, or those famous white cliffs of Dover. Or even milk! But isn't that the whole point of drinking all that milk—to build strong bones and teeth with calcium? Or is it just to wash down a gigantic plate of brownies?

First of all, calcium is a metal, so you won't be too surprised to learn that in its pure form it is firm, shiny, and a bit silvery. But the second thing to remember is that calcium is in column 2 of the periodic table, so it's part of the alkaline earth metal group. Just think of magnesium (see page 99), and you'll at least have an idea of how pure calcium looks.

So where does that "white as the driven snow" business come into it? That also comes down to calcium's position on the periodic table. It reacts well with other elements and forms compounds easily, and it's those compounds that are often white. The white powder that the lifeguard tosses into the pool each evening? Chances are it's calcium hypochlorite. A toothpaste that promises whiter teeth? It probably contains tricalcium phosphate.

WHEN WAS CALCIUM DISCOVERED?

The name "calcium" comes from the Latin word *calx*, which means "lime." That's not the stuff in your Key lime pie, though. It's the kind of lime used as the main ingredient of white plaster on walls, for instance. This lime is a calcium compound—calcium carbonate ($CaCO_3$)— which is used to make building mortar. Another name for this compound is limestone. Have you ever seen pictures of the Colosseum in Rome? That was built with calx and stone more than 1,900 years ago and (most of it) is still going strong.

That wasn't the only calcium compound that ancient people found useful. Although the Romans didn't know the chemistry behind some of their techniques, they knew that by heating limestone they would get an even better building material, which they could mix with water to make cement. Nowadays we would say that by heating the limestone ($CaCO_3$) the Romans got rid of the carbon dioxide (CO_2). What was left was calcium oxide (CaO)... which mixed with the water to become cement. The one constant in all of these, of course, is the element calcium (Ca).

The actual discovery of pure calcium is a story of generosity and cooperation. British scientist Sir Humphry Davy—one of the greatest element hunters in history—managed to isolate a small amount of calcium in 1808. He announced his breakthrough to Britain's leading scientific organization, the Royal Society, noting how extremely difficult it was to obtain even a small calcium sample in his experiments.

Then Davy received a letter from Sweden. It was from Jöns Berzelius, a skilled chemist. This Swedish colleague pointed out how it was possible to run an electrical current through mercury oxide and calcium oxide. The process separated the oxygen (oxide) from each compound and produced a mixture of mercury and calcium. That was enough to enable Davy to separate these two elements—and produce better amounts of calcium.

WHERE IS CALCIUM USED?

When you're next at the chalkboard, trying to remember how to spell "Mediterranean," remember that chalk has a long history. The Anglo-Saxons living in England from about 500 CE referred to calcium carbonate (chalk) as *hwiting-melu*, which meant "whitening powder." It is the whiteness of many calcium compounds as much as their cementing qualities that has made them attractive over the years, because many people believed that the bright color was a reminder of heaven.

Those are still important uses of calcium compounds, sometimes coupled with another quality that calcium provides: alkalinity, just like magnesium (see page 99). On its own, or more commonly, bonded with other elements, calcium neutralizes acids. For example, fertilizers containing calcium help rebalance acidic soils so farmers can grow crops again.

Calcium's ability to bond easily has led to tons of industrial uses. It is an effective tool in extracting some metals, such as thorium and uranium (see page 232), from their compounds. Calcium also draws nonmetal impurities from metals and alloys, and combined with chlorine (to make calcium chloride) it's an excellent de-icer for snowy days.

So how about all that cow juice full of calcium you're encouraged to drink? That's because calcium combined with phosphorus becomes the strength that our skeletons need to keep us standing. But bones don't just stay as they are inside our bodies: They are constantly being broken down and rebuilt—and that rebuilding calls for more calcium. Nerve cells and muscles also rely on calcium, and if they run low, the body will look to the nearest "calcium storeroom"—our bones—to get new supplies. If we can't keep pace with this loss of calcium, our bones become weaker.

BARIUM: A NOT-SO-TASTY MEAL

1 H																	2 He
3 Li	4 Be											5 B	6 C	7 N	8 O	9 F	10 Ne
11 Na	12 Mg											13 Al	14 Si	15 P	16 S	17 Cl	18 Ar
19 K	20 Ca	21 Sc	22 Ti	23 V	24 Cr	25 Mn	26 Fe	27 Co	28 Ni	29 Cu	30 Zn	31 Ga	32 Ge	33 As	34 Se	35 Br	36 Kr
37 Rb	38 Sr	39 Y	40 Zr	41 Nb	42 Mo	43 Tc	44 Ru	45 Rh	46 Pd	47 Ag	48 Cd	49 In	50 Sn	51 Sb	52 Te	53 I	54 Xe
55 Cs	56 Ba		72 Hf	73 Ta	74 W	75 Re	76 Os	77 Ir	78 Pt	79 Au	80 Hg	81 Tl	82 Pb	83 Bi	84 Po	85 At	86 Rn
87 Fr	88 Ra		104 Rf	105 Db	106 Sg	107 Bh	108 Hs	109 Mt	110 Ds	111 Rg	112 Cn	113 Nh	114 Fl	115 Mc	116 Lv	117 Ts	118 Og

57 La	58 Ce	59 Pr	60 Nd	61 Pm	62 Sm	63 Eu	64 Gd	65 Tb	66 Dy	67 Ho	68 Er	69 Tm	70 Yb	71 Lu
89 Ac	90 Th	91 Pa	92 U	93 Np	94 Pu	95 Am	96 Cm	97 Bk	98 Cf	99 Es	100 Fm	101 Md	102 No	103 Lr

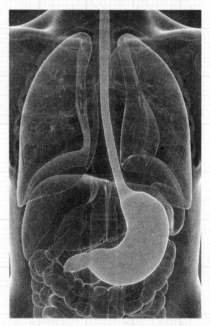

The stomach and areas around it don't show up well on X-rays, which makes it harder for doctors to notice problems such as ulcers (holes in the stomach lining). One of calcium's relatives, the element barium (Ba), which is two rows down group 2, can come to the rescue. Barium is also an alkaline earth metal, and it's very dense. Unlike the soft tissue in that part of your body, barium does show up clearly on an X-ray, so if doctors coat the inside of your stomach with barium, they can get a good picture of what's there.

They call this sort of procedure a barium meal. First they make sure that you haven't eaten for a few hours and that your stomach is empty. Then you drink about three cups of a barium-based drink. It tastes a bit chalky—not surprising, considering that barium is a relative of calcium—but extra flavors can mask the taste. Then, within a few minutes, your stomach has been coated on the inside and they're ready to take the X-rays. Yummy!

DANGER LEVEL

☢ ☢ ☢ ☢ ☢

Considering calcium's importance for our health, it's the *lack* of calcium that is dangerous rather than the element itself. If the body uses up more calcium than it takes in, then it could develop weakened bones—a condition called osteoporosis.

So how do you avoid this danger—especially if you're sick of drinking all that milk? Well, you could try to get your share of calcium from cabbage. No? How about broccoli? Red kidney beans? OK, you could always try milk chocolate!

 **EXPERIMENT** *with the* **ELEMENT**

"You can't turn back the clock," you often hear people say. They mean you can't "unbreak" the window that you just hit with a baseball or "repour" the milk that you spilled on the floor. But you can put some experiments into reverse, including this one involving calcium.

NOT SUCH A SOFTIE

Stage 1 of this experiment might be familiar to you—it's a way of demonstrating how the acid in vinegar eats away at the shell of an egg. The result usually gets oohs and aahs and a few laughs.

But Stage 2 is where the real magic happens. It tries to turn the clock back to get the shell hard again. And who's behind that plan? Well, it's the element calcium.

YOU WILL NEED

- ◆ **2 cups (about 500 ml) of vinegar**
- ◆ **A glass or jar**
- ◆ **Uncooked egg**
- ◆ **Saucer**

METHOD

1 Pour the vinegar into the glass or jar.

2 Carefully add the egg, but tap it lightly with your finger first to remind yourself of how hard it is.

3 Leave the egg in the vinegar for a day.

4 Tip the jar to carefully pour out the liquid, then remove the egg and tap it: The outside should be much softer. You've just completed Stage 1 of the "rubber egg" demonstration.

5 Now for Stage 2: Leave the egg on the saucer on a table or counter for another day.

6 Test the outside again. Has it become harder?

HEY, WHAT'S GOING ON?

Stage 1 of the experiment saw the acid of the vinegar reacting with the shell of the egg. That shell is made of calcium carbonate. You could see the reaction taking place as small bubbles floated away from the egg. They were carbon dioxide. The reaction continued until all of the carbon in the shell was used up. By then the shell was pretty soft. Importantly, though, not all of the calcium (from the calcium carbonate) had been used up.

Stage 2 gave that remaining calcium the chance to bond with more carbon to build some more calcium carbonate again. And where does it find that carbon? Well, take a breath and you'll find some, too. That's right, it got some from the air, which has lots of carbon dioxide.

ATOMIC NUMBER: 26	ELECTRONS IN OUTERMOST SHELL: 2*
ATOMIC WEIGHT: 55.845	MELTING POINT: 2,800°F (1,538°C)
ELEMENT SYMBOL: Fe	BOILING POINT: 5,182°F (2,861°C)

CHAPTER 17

* Transition metals have a different method of counting valence electrons (see "Meet the Relatives" on page 178).

IRON

¹ H																	² He
³ Li	⁴ Be											⁵ B	⁶ C	⁷ N	⁸ O	⁹ F	¹⁰ Ne
¹¹ Na	¹² Mg											¹³ Al	¹⁴ Si	¹⁵ P	¹⁶ S	¹⁷ Cl	¹⁸ Ar
¹⁹ K	²⁰ Ca	²¹ Sc	²² Ti	²³ V	²⁴ Cr	²⁵ Mn	²⁶ Fe	²⁷ Co	²⁸ Ni	²⁹ Cu	³⁰ Zn	³¹ Ga	³² Ge	³³ As	³⁴ Se	³⁵ Br	³⁶ Kr
³⁷ Rb	³⁸ Sr	³⁹ Y	⁴⁰ Zr	⁴¹ Nb	⁴² Mo	⁴³ Tc	⁴⁴ Ru	⁴⁵ Rh	⁴⁶ Pd	⁴⁷ Ag	⁴⁸ Cd	⁴⁹ In	⁵⁰ Sn	⁵¹ Sb	⁵² Te	⁵³ I	⁵⁴ Xe
⁵⁵ Cs	⁵⁶ Ba		⁷² Hf	⁷³ Ta	⁷⁴ W	⁷⁵ Re	⁷⁶ Os	⁷⁷ Ir	⁷⁸ Pt	⁷⁹ Au	⁸⁰ Hg	⁸¹ Tl	⁸² Pb	⁸³ Bi	⁸⁴ Po	⁸⁵ At	⁸⁶ Rn
⁸⁷ Fr	⁸⁸ Ra		¹⁰⁴ Rf	¹⁰⁵ Db	¹⁰⁶ Sg	¹⁰⁷ Bh	¹⁰⁸ Hs	¹⁰⁹ Mt	¹¹⁰ Ds	¹¹¹ Rg	¹¹² Cn	¹¹³ Nh	¹¹⁴ Fl	¹¹⁵ Mc	¹¹⁶ Lv	¹¹⁷ Ts	¹¹⁸ Og

⁵⁷ La	⁵⁸ Ce	⁵⁹ Pr	⁶⁰ Nd	⁶¹ Pm	⁶² Sm	⁶³ Eu	⁶⁴ Gd	⁶⁵ Tb	⁶⁶ Dy	⁶⁷ Ho	⁶⁸ Er	⁶⁹ Tm	⁷⁰ Yb	⁷¹ Lu
⁸⁹ Ac	⁹⁰ Th	⁹¹ Pa	⁹² U	⁹³ Np	⁹⁴ Pu	⁹⁵ Am	⁹⁶ Cm	⁹⁷ Bk	⁹⁸ Cf	⁹⁹ Es	¹⁰⁰ Fm	¹⁰¹ Md	¹⁰² No	¹⁰³ Lr

Some elements need no introduction because, well, their reputation is already so well established that we know they're really important. And they don't come much more important than iron.

It's an element that the ancient Egyptians believed was a gift from the gods. A substance that revolutionized how people made tools, vehicles, and weapons. A synonym for strength, essential for every red blood cell in your body, the heart of skyscrapers, and the only element with an age named for it, iron is a superstar in the periodic table—and the universe.

Yet, despite its power and versatility, iron can be brought to its knees (or broken down) by being exposed to oxygen.

Then again, if you add just a little impurity to it as you're melting it down, the new mixture can get even stronger. So who would win: Iron Man or the Man of Steel? Read on.

WHAT DOES IRON LOOK LIKE?

Pure iron is a solid, silvery-gray metal at room temperature. It is ductile, meaning that it can be formed into a thin wire. But you've probably come across the chemical reaction that takes place when iron is exposed to air and water: It rusts (oxidizes), flaking off and becoming weaker. The reddish-brown flakes that result are known as oxides.

Luckily iron can be turned into much harder steel, and it forms alloys with other metals easily. This wide range of mixtures means that iron can be put to use in many, many ways.

WHEN WAS IRON DISCOVERED?

Here's an element that doesn't have a known discoverer. Why? Well, because it has been used for about 7,000 years. For something that's so useful and widespread now, iron is hard to find in its pure form. The people who first found and used iron all those years ago almost certainly got it from meteorites that had crashed into Earth from space and contained large amounts of iron. The iron beads and necklaces found in Egyptian tombs were probably made from that source. In fact, the Egyptians called iron *ba-ne-pe*, which meant "metal from heaven." Hmm . . .

OK, so there's not a whole lot of pure iron lying around. Unless you count the 4,350-mile-wide core of planet Earth, which is made of iron. But there are tons—hundreds of millions of tons—of it locked in ores on the Earth's surface or just underground. And people have been smelting that ore (applying extreme heat and chemicals to release the pure metal inside) for about 3,500 years, probably starting in what is now Turkey.

That was the beginning of the Iron Age, which took its name from the wide range of tools and weapons made from this metal. But there's a funny thing about iron. It had already made a name for itself as a "tough guy," but if an impurity got mixed in during the smelting process, the iron got even tougher.

One of the obvious things to get mixed in would have been charcoal, since the smelting process called for constant heat, and charcoal would have been the fuel of choice. But remember that charcoal is simply carbon, so mixing it with iron was a way of mixing two elements. And it's the carbon-iron combination that produced the really strong and durable metal: steel. Steel contains between 0.2 and 2.1 percent carbon, yet it's the carbon that gives steel its strength.

If you thought that this chapter was one in which the names Sir Humphry Davy and Antoine Lavoisier wouldn't crop up, you'd be right. By the time those two busy chemists were around, iron had been in use—and fully documented—for centuries.

WHERE IS IRON USED?

By the time of the ancient Greeks and Romans, iron was being used in all walks of life. (Its symbol, Fe, comes from the Latin word for iron—*ferrum*.) The Roman historian Pliny the Elder, writing nearly 2,000 years ago, observed, "It is by the aid of iron that we construct houses, cleave (break apart) rocks, and perform so many other useful offices in life."

Pliny was one smart dude—he also seemed to be able to look into the future, at least as far as iron was concerned. Do you think any of this could be describing wars in the 20th and 21st centuries? He wrote, "With iron, wars take place, and not only hand-to-hand but from a distance, with winged weapons launched from engines."

Nowadays, we are accustomed to seeing iron all around us. It is by far the least expensive and most widely used metal, accounting for about 95 percent of all metal production in the world. The secret of iron's success—apart from its abundance and low cost—is the remarkable variety of ways that it can be formed, bent, or forged into useful shapes.

On top of all that, iron is a cornerstone of human health. It is a life-giver, transporting oxygen (in red blood cells) to every part of your body. (Pretty cool to think that little bits of metal are inside all of us, isn't it?) And iron's attraction to magnets (and the way that iron itself can become a magnet) is an important—and still slightly mysterious—feature of the element. Scientists now believe that birds pick up magnetic signals from inside the Earth to guide them on their long journeys through the air.

Meet the Relatives 🤝

TRANSITION METALS:
PLAYING TO DIFFERENT RULES

1 H																	2 He
3 Li	4 Be											5 B	6 C	7 N	8 O	9 F	10 Ne
11 Na	12 Mg											13 Al	14 Si	15 P	16 S	17 Cl	18 Ar
19 K	20 Ca	21 Sc	22 Ti	23 V	24 Cr	25 Mn	26 Fe	27 Co	28 Ni	29 Cu	30 Zn	31 Ga	32 Ge	33 As	34 Se	35 Br	36 Kr
37 Rb	38 Sr	39 Y	40 Zr	41 Nb	42 Mo	43 Tc	44 Ru	45 Rh	46 Pd	47 Ag	48 Cd	49 In	50 Sn	51 Sb	52 Te	53 I	54 Xe
55 Cs	56 Ba		72 Hf	73 Ta	74 W	75 Re	76 Os	77 Ir	78 Pt	79 Au	80 Hg	81 Tl	82 Pb	83 Bi	84 Po	85 At	86 Rn
87 Fr	88 Ra		104 Rf	105 Db	106 Sg	107 Bh	108 Hs	109 Mt	110 Ds	111 Rg	112 Cn	113 Nh	114 Fl	115 Mc	116 Lv	117 Ts	118 Og

57 La	58 Ce	59 Pr	60 Nd	61 Pm	62 Sm	63 Eu	64 Gd	65 Tb	66 Dy	67 Ho	68 Er	69 Tm	70 Yb	71 Lu
89 Ac	90 Th	91 Pa	92 U	93 Np	94 Pu	95 Am	96 Cm	97 Bk	98 Cf	99 Es	100 Fm	101 Md	102 No	103 Lr

OK. Here's a confession. Up to now, all the elements that you've been reading about have fallen in columns 1, 2, or 13 to 18 of the periodic table. And one of the neat things about those elements is that the last digit of their column is the same as the number of outer-shell (valence) electrons they have. Together, they're known as the main group elements. But with iron, hanging out there in column 8, we have the first example of a transition metal.

The transition metals sit in columns 3 to 12 of the periodic table. They fill their electron shells differently, so the octet rule doesn't apply. You'll need some more classroom chemistry—about how electron shells can even have *sub*shells—to learn just how these metals behave so specially. But in the meantime, you can get a glimpse of that behavior in iron and in the next two chapters' elements (copper and zinc).

DANGER LEVEL

It's pretty obvious that iron can be used to make some awfully dangerous stuff. Of course, weapons like iron cannonballs and rifles raise the danger levels even higher. An element as strong, sturdy, versatile — and common — as iron will always have dangers associated with it along with its contributions to human life. But what about other dangers? You won't be surprised to learn that not having enough iron in your diet can cause a number of dangers. One of the worst of those dangers is not being able to learn things as easily. It's harder to have too much iron, but that can lead to other problems. Usually it's children, not adults, who wind up with too much iron, so be very, very careful when you take vitamins — and make sure a grownup is there to keep track of what you've taken. Too much iron can lead to stomachaches and constipation, but a very high dose could be fatal.

EXPERIMENT *with the* ELEMENT

Har-har-har, my mateys. You are about to be punished with sizzling, red-hot iron—prepare to breathe your last! What's that you say—"exothermic"? We'll have none of those big scientific words around here, matey!

BURNING IRON

Yes, this experiment really *is* about iron in a rising temperature, but don't worry—you won't be breathing your last. You will, however, be noticing an aspect of a chemical reaction that you don't normally notice.

YOU WILL NEED

- **Steel wool (either rolled or pads, but *not* filled with soap)**
- **Glass or mug**
- **White vinegar**
- **"Stick" thermometer**
- **Glass jar with lid—ideally tall and narrow**
- **Pen and paper**

METHOD

1 Take a steel wool pad or tear off a piece of steel wool about 5 inches (13 cm) long.

2 Put the steel wool in the glass or mug.

3 Fill the mug with vinegar and leave it alone for a minute.

4 Take the steel wool out and wring out the excess vinegar.

5 Insert the base of the thermometer into the pad or roll it up in the piece of steel wool.

6 Place the steel wool and thermometer in the jar so that you can read the temperature.

7 Close the lid and note the temperature.

8 Write down the temperature every minute for 10 minutes.

HEY, WHAT'S GOING ON?

The first stage allowed the acid in the vinegar to eat away at the protective substances on the surface of the steel wool. That meant that the iron (part of the steel) was exposed to the air and could react with the oxygen in it. That process, known as oxidation, is also called rust. (You'd recognize the results pretty soon anyway, because we all know how iron discolors as it rusts.) But the oxidation reaction is also exothermic, meaning it gives off heat. And that's why the temperature should rise (especially as you are trapping the heat with the lid).

Wait a minute. "Needs oxygen for the reaction?" "Gives off heat?" That sounds a bit like a blazing fire. Yep, the results of your experiment could really be described as "burning iron," even if that burning is a slow-motion version compared to a blaze in a fireplace.

ATOMIC NUMBER: 29	ELECTRONS IN OUTERMOST SHELL: 2*
ATOMIC WEIGHT: 63.546	MELTING POINT: 1,843.2°F (1,084.62°C)
ELEMENT SYMBOL: Cu	BOILING POINT: 4,643°F (2,562°C)

CHAPTER 18

* Transition metals have a different method of counting valence electrons (see "Meet the Relatives" on page 178).

1 H																	2 He
3 Li	4 Be											5 B	6 C	7 N	8 O	9 F	10 Ne
11 Na	12 Mg											13 Al	14 Si	15 P	16 S	17 Cl	18 Ar
19 K	20 Ca	21 Sc	22 Ti	23 V	24 Cr	25 Mn	26 Fe	27 Co	28 Ni	29 Cu	30 Zn	31 Ga	32 Ge	33 As	34 Se	35 Br	36 Kr
37 Rb	38 Sr	39 Y	40 Zr	41 Nb	42 Mo	43 Tc	44 Ru	45 Rh	46 Pd	47 Ag	48 Cd	49 In	50 Sn	51 Sb	52 Te	53 I	54 Xe
55 Cs	56 Ba		72 Hf	73 Ta	74 W	75 Re	76 Os	77 Ir	78 Pt	79 Au	80 Hg	81 Tl	82 Pb	83 Bi	84 Po	85 At	86 Rn
87 Fr	88 Ra		104 Rf	105 Db	106 Sg	107 Bh	108 Hs	109 Mt	110 Ds	111 Rg	112 Cn	113 Nh	114 Fl	115 Mc	116 Lv	117 Ts	118 Og

57 La	58 Ce	59 Pr	60 Nd	61 Pm	62 Sm	63 Eu	64 Gd	65 Tb	66 Dy	67 Ho	68 Er	69 Tm	70 Yb	71 Lu
89 Ac	90 Th	91 Pa	92 U	93 Np	94 Pu	95 Am	96 Cm	97 Bk	98 Cf	99 Es	100 Fm	101 Md	102 No	103 Lr

Think of gold or silver, and you immediately come up with images of wealth — kings counting coins in palaces, or Spanish ships returning from the New World with Aztec and Incan riches. What sort of image springs to mind for copper? Those "take one" boxes of pennies beside cash registers, where people can dump unwanted copper pennies? A bit of copper pipe under the sink?

Sure, you'd probably rather have a piggy bank full of gold or silver coins than copper pennies, but imagine how much it would cost if your house were wired with one of those metals? Or how you'd feel cooking pancakes on a gold or silver frying pan?

No, copper doesn't have to apologize at all. And anyway, all you have to do is mix it with tin (see page 202), and you get bronze—and that's the name of an important age in history. Anyone ever heard of the Gold Age or the Silver Age? Nope!

WHAT DOES COPPER LOOK LIKE?

Here's where copper gets a chance to stand out. It's a metal element that *doesn't* look silvery gray. Of the hundred or so metals in the periodic table, only two other elements can make that claim: gold and cesium. So if it's not silver or gray, then what color is it? It's a distinctive reddish-orange color that we call, well, copper. In fact, some think the word "cop" (meaning police officer) comes from the copper buttons of the earliest police uniforms.

Copper is robust, and although it does oxidize (react with oxygen in the damp air), it doesn't really break down the way iron does when it rusts. Instead, it forms the compound copper oxide, which actually acts as a shield against further oxidation. This greenish compound is sometimes called patina, and you can see it on the surface of the Statue of Liberty and other places where copper is exposed to the air.

WHEN WAS COPPER DISCOVERED?

Copper may not have the glamorous image of some other metals, but it does have a history—a long history—and has been helping humans in all sort of ways for up to 10,000 years. It was probably the first metal that humans worked with, apart from the iron that was contained in meteorites.

Evidence from the Middle East indicates that ancient miners broke copper ore from rocks, crushed it, and roasted it in furnaces that reached copper's melting point of 1,843.2°F. (Ash from these archaeological sites suggests they burned charcoal to achieve that heat.) The melted copper would be poured out and cooled, and the process was repeated several times to remove impurities. Eventually it would be poured into stone molds to form all sorts of weapons, jewelry, and tools.

By the time of the ancient Romans, most copper was mined on the Mediterranean island of Cyprus. The modern symbol for the element, Cu, reflects that history: It was originally called *aes Cyprium* ("metal from Cyprus"), which was shortened to *cuprum*.

WHERE IS COPPER USED?

Apart from being the first metal to be mined and used by humans, copper has proved to be one of the most useful. It is malleable (can be bent into shape easily), ductile (can be formed into thin wires), and a good conductor of electricity. Those three qualities combine to make it an obvious choice for electrical wiring.

A CLUE IN THE ICE

In September 1991, two hikers in the Italian Alps reported finding the frozen body of an unfortunate climber who must have died a few years earlier. It soon became clear that this wasn't a matter for the police, but for archaeologists. Tests revealed that Ötzi the Iceman (named after the Ötzital Alps, where he was found) had been preserved in ice for more than 5,000 years.

Everything about him was studied to shed light on life so many years ago. The most important find? His copper-headed ax. Scientists conducted tests with a similar ax and found that it could fell a full-size tree in just over half an hour—not bad for five millennia ago. The ax revealed more about the man himself, too. At that time, only chieftains and high-ranking warriors had tools and weapons made from precious copper. Would that explain why he was so high up in the mountains, though? One theory is that he was a tribal leader who was also a prospector . . . looking for more copper.

Copper also conducts heat very well and doesn't tarnish (lose its shine because of a chemical reaction). That makes it ideal for pots and pans. Villedieu-les-Poêles, a town in northern France (its name means "God's town of the frying pans"), has become world-famous for its cooking equipment—all made from copper. But copper isn't confined to the kitchen. Just think of where it keeps cropping up—electrical wiring, saxophones, and even the 80 tons of it that were cut and hammered to construct the Statue of Liberty.

Either on its own—using its conducting powers—or alloyed with other metals, copper is used in hundreds of ways. It really lies at the heart of modern life, because copper wires play a vital role in the generation and transmission of electricity. It even works behind the scenes: The element nickel only makes up a quarter of the nickel coin that you get in change. The other 75 percent? Copper.

Meet the Relatives

COINAGE METALS: VALUABLE NEIGHBORS?

Copper's next-door neighbor on the fourth row (period) of the periodic table is nickel (Ni). When you consider that most US pennies were made of copper for many years, it's not surprising that the namesake of the next-highest coin would be so close. But if you

look down the column from copper, you notice two more examples of why group 11 is called coinage elements. There they are: precious silver (Ag) and gold (Au). This must be the fancy-shmancy neighborhood of the table.

But just how valuable are they? Well, all of these metals are traded, and their price per ton goes up and down, just like the value of the dollar or of stocks and shares. Here's a snapshot of what each metal was worth at the beginning of 2018. Each price is for a ton of the metal.

| COPPER → $7,440 | NICKEL → $13,910 |
| SILVER → $640,000 | GOLD → $39,168,000 |

DANGER LEVEL

☢ ☢ ☢ ☢ ☢

Copper is one of the safest elements, and in many ways it is better known for protecting against danger. Harmful disease-carrying organisms called microbes (see page 204) don't survive well on copper surfaces, which is why many hospitals have copper doorknobs and closet handles. Copper forms chemical reactions with some of the proteins, fats, and other chemical ingredients of the microbes, making it hard for the microbes to reproduce or in some cases killing them outright.

EXPERIMENT *with the* ELEMENT

The next experiment is pretty . . . well, there's no word to describe it other than "weird." You'll probably agree, but you're just as likely to say "cool" or "awesome." It's one of the experiments in the book that will require you to buy something, but you'll agree it's worth it.

MAY THE FORCE BE WITH YOU

Most of the ingredients for the experiments in this book can be found around your house. This one, though, calls for two ingredients that you might not have at home. Still, it won't be wasted money. You can always use the copper pipe if you have a plumbing emergency.

And the other—well, that's the cool one, so you won't mind keeping that either. It's called a neodymium magnet, and you should be able to buy one or two nearby at a hardware store.

So should you go to the trouble to get hold of these special ingredients? You'll soon see—literally, since the experiment only takes an instant. But the result is magical, since you will be defying gravity, or at least seeming to slow it down. It's all down to the power of electromagnetic forces.

YOU WILL NEED

- ◆ 3- to 4-foot (0.9 to 1.2 m) length of copper pipe (about ¾-inch or 1.9 cm diameter—the sort used in plumbing)
- ◆ 1 or 2 disk-shaped neodymium magnets (almost but not quite as wide as the diameter of the pipe)

METHOD

 Hold the pipe upright, but low enough that you can look down it.

 Take a magnet (or two stuck together) and hold it at the top of the pipe.

3 Drop the magnet and observe.

4 It should seem to float down the pipe rather than fall.

HEY, WHAT'S GOING ON?

Copper conducts electricity very well, but it isn't known for its magnetic properties. If you put a magnet up to a sheet of copper it probably wouldn't stick, but if you enlist the aid of another element, neodymium (Nd), things start to change. Neodymium magnets are the most powerful permanent magnets that are generally available. They're actually made of an alloy of three elements—neodymium, iron, and boron—which combine to create a crystal structure with a very strong magnetic field. (Don't forget: Magnetism and electricity are related.)

In this experiment, the powerful magnetic field of the falling neodymium magnet creates an electrical current (called an eddy current) in the copper. And that copper current, in turn, produces its own magnetic field, because electricity and magnetism are closely related. The two fields overlap, causing the falling magnet to slow down.

ATOMIC NUMBER: 30	ELECTRONS IN OUTERMOST SHELL: 2*
ATOMIC WEIGHT: 65.409	MELTING POINT: 787.15°F (419.53°C)
ELEMENT SYMBOL: Zn	BOILING POINT: 1,665°F (907°C)

CHAPTER 19

ZINC

* Transition metals have a different method of counting valence electrons (see "Meet the Relatives" on page 178).

1 H																	2 He
3 Li	4 Be											5 B	6 C	7 N	8 O	9 F	10 Ne
11 Na	12 Mg											13 Al	14 Si	15 P	16 S	17 Cl	18 Ar
19 K	20 Ca	21 Sc	22 Ti	23 V	24 Cr	25 Mn	26 Fe	27 Co	28 Ni	29 Cu	30 Zn	31 Ga	32 Ge	33 As	34 Se	35 Br	36 Kr
37 Rb	38 Sr	39 Y	40 Zr	41 Nb	42 Mo	43 Tc	44 Ru	45 Rh	46 Pd	47 Ag	48 Cd	49 In	50 Sn	51 Sb	52 Te	53 I	54 Xe
55 Cs	56 Ba		72 Hf	73 Ta	74 W	75 Re	76 Os	77 Ir	78 Pt	79 Au	80 Hg	81 Tl	82 Pb	83 Bi	84 Po	85 At	86 Rn
87 Fr	88 Ra		104 Rf	105 Db	106 Sg	107 Bh	108 Hs	109 Mt	110 Ds	111 Rg	112 Cn	113 Nh	114 Fl	115 Mc	116 Lv	117 Ts	118 Og

	57 La	58 Ce	59 Pr	60 Nd	61 Pm	62 Sm	63 Eu	64 Gd	65 Tb	66 Dy	67 Ho	68 Er	69 Tm	70 Yb	71 Lu
	89 Ac	90 Th	91 Pa	92 U	93 Np	94 Pu	95 Am	96 Cm	97 Bk	98 Cf	99 Es	100 Fm	101 Md	102 No	103 Lr

"**L**eaves of three, let them be."

If you've ever ignored that very good advice and ended up in a bunch of poison ivy, you might've used calamine lotion to help soothe the burn. That pink, creamy stuff works for sunburn, rashes, chickenpox, and insect stings as well. But did you know that the element zinc is the main ingredient in calamine lotion, in the form of its compound zinc oxide (ZnO)? And that years ago, your mother or father probably used it to soothe your diaper rash? (You probably don't even want to think about *that*.)

But zinc isn't just important for soothing skin and to stop babies' tears. It's essential for your growth and development, not to mention your digestion and ability to fight disease and infection. And that's just part of the way zinc proves itself over and over for human well-being. Remember how a bit of carbon added to iron made it into a much harder combo—steel? Well, even steel needs some help against rust and corrosion. And that's where zinc comes in. Oh, and by the way—brass is an alloy of copper and . . . zinc.

WHAT DOES ZINC LOOK LIKE?

Zinc is a bluish-white or bluish-silver solid metal. It is quite brittle at room temperature, but it becomes more malleable (able to be bent into different shapes) at temperatures above the boiling point of water (212°F/100°C).

It's very rare to come across zinc in this natural state; normally it's found in ores such as sphalerite (a mixture of zinc, sulfur, and iron) and calamine (zinc, oxygen, iron, and sometimes carbon). How these ores look depends on the elements that make them up. Most of us, though, will recognize zinc from its most famous alloy, brass. Trumpets, tubas, and trombones are all made of the stuff.

WHEN WAS ZINC DISCOVERED?

Zinc, in its various compounds, has been known for thousands of years, but these compounds were rarely studied or used. Things changed around a thousand years ago when it began to be smelted in China and India. Increased trade with Asia introduced Europeans to these metals, prompting scientists to explore for new elements. In 1746, German chemist Andreas Marggraf isolated pure zinc and identified it, securing its place as an element in its own right.

Some people claim that the name "zinc" comes from an old German word, *zinke*, meaning "pointed." It refers to the pointed crystals that zinc formed after it was smelted. Others disagree, saying that it's closer to an old Persian word *sing*, meaning "stone."

ANDREAS MARGGRAF

TRACE ELEMENT

Zinc is often described as an important trace element for plants and animals (including humans). A trace element is necessary for life, although not in as high concentrations as other elements. For example, human beings (like all mammals) need lots of carbon, hydrogen, oxygen, and nitrogen. These elements keep our "engines" running.

Other much-needed elements include calcium, phosphorus, potassium, sulfur, sodium, magnesium, and chlorine. Our bodies also need tiny amounts of other elements — zinc, as well as iron, copper, iodine, and a few others — to perform specialized jobs in our cells.

WHERE IS ZINC USED?

As a relatively inexpensive metal, zinc is pretty useful—
especially for the United States Mint, which is responsible
for producing the nation's coins. Most people think of
the one-cent coin (the penny) as being copper, and for a
brief period in US history (1793–1837), the cent was pure
copper. Zinc crept in, along with tin and later nickel, to
make up 5 percent of the coin's composition.

Then something strange happened. The value of the
cent declined while the value of copper rose. By the early
1980s, the amount of copper in a penny was worth more
than a cent. The government was losing money with
every one-cent coin! So, since 1983, every cent has been
made of 95 percent zinc, with a coating of copper making up the other 5 percent.

OK, so zinc may not at first seem as exciting as
expensive gold or explosive phosphorous. After all, you
don't hear of catastrophic zinc explosions, or zinc mil-
lionaires, or daring zinc robberies too often. Well, maybe

you should consider what many people think of as the world's most beautiful, romantic city—Paris. A view from the Eiffel Tower extends across the rooftops of Paris, which have inspired poets and artists since the 1860s, when local laws insisted that all new roofs be covered with rolled zinc. The Parisians must really love that element, because the bars in most cafés are also covered in rolled zinc. And when French people go to the bar, they say that they're going to *le zinc*.

GALLIUM: TRIUMPH FOR MENDELEEV

1 H																	2 He
3 Li	4 Be											5 B	6 C	7 N	8 O	9 F	10 Ne
11 Na	12 Mg											13 Al	14 Si	15 P	16 S	17 Cl	18 Ar
19 K	20 Ca	21 Sc	22 Ti	23 V	24 Cr	25 Mn	26 Fe	27 Co	28 Ni	29 Cu	30 Zn	31 Ga	32 Ge	33 As	34 Se	35 Br	36 Kr
37 Rb	38 Sr	39 Y	40 Zr	41 Nb	42 Mo	43 Tc	44 Ru	45 Rh	46 Pd	47 Ag	48 Cd	49 In	50 Sn	51 Sb	52 Te	53 I	54 Xe
55 Cs	56 Ba		72 Hf	73 Ta	74 W	75 Re	76 Os	77 Ir	78 Pt	79 Au	80 Hg	81 Tl	82 Pb	83 Bi	84 Po	85 At	86 Rn
87 Fr	88 Ra		104 Rf	105 Db	106 Sg	107 Bh	108 Hs	109 Mt	110 Ds	111 Rg	112 Cn	113 Nh	114 Fl	115 Mc	116 Lv	117 Ts	118 Og

57 La	58 Ce	59 Pr	60 Nd	61 Pm	62 Sm	63 Eu	64 Gd	65 Tb	66 Dy	67 Ho	68 Er	69 Tm	70 Yb	71 Lu
89 Ac	90 Th	91 Pa	92 U	93 Np	94 Pu	95 Am	96 Cm	97 Bk	98 Cf	99 Es	100 Fm	101 Md	102 No	103 Lr

As you read about all of these elements, make sure to give credit to our old pal Dmitri Mendeleev, the Russian scientist who developed the periodic table in the 19th century. It was plenty impressive to arrange all the known elements in crisscrossed patterns (periods and groups), but he went further. Mendeleev left blanks for elements that he knew must exist but hadn't found yet.

The element we know as gallium (Ga) was the first to prove the great scientist right—and in his lifetime. Mendeleev left a blank to the right of zinc. The blank space was waiting for an element with atomic number 31. Why there? Because he correctly predicted that the unknown element would bond with other elements— just like the known element right above it, aluminum (Al)—because they had the same number of outer-shell electrons.

In 1875, Paul-Emile Lecoq de Boisbaudran of France discovered an element that matched Mendeleev's predictions almost exactly. He named it gallium, after the Latin name for France, *Gallia*.

ZINC ON THE MENU

Many foods are high in zinc, such as red meat, shellfish, spinach, dairy products, and even maple syrup. These foods are not common in some of the most zinc-deficient countries, especially in Asia, where rice is the main crop. United Nations agencies are finding new ways to introduce zinc into the soil in these areas. Farmers will benefit because the extra zinc could boost harvests by as much as 30 percent. Local people will also find improvements in their health.

DANGER LEVEL

☢ ☢ ☢ ☢ ☢

The dangers linked to zinc have less to do with touching it or having it explode than to its role in the human body. And it's a *lack* of zinc, rather than too much of it, that is more likely to cause concern. "Zinc deficiency" can lead to stunted growth, diarrhea, pneumonia, and even cancer. This deficiency is far more common in the developing world (countries that have little modern industry); some scientists estimate that 800,000 people die each year because they don't get enough zinc in their diet or in supplements.

EXPERIMENT *with the* ELEMENT

Like tin (see page 201), zinc is often used to protect other metals from rusting. This process is called galvanization, and it involves coating the other metal with a thin layer of zinc. Nails are often galvanized—for obvious reasons—and you'll be using two of them to help power this experiment.

DID YOU WIND THE POTATO CLOCK?

The answer is NO, because you're the one supplying the power. Or perhaps we should say that it's two potatoes supplying the power. Or more precisely, the zinc-coated nails stuck into those two potatoes. Or better still—the electrons flowing from the zinc-coated nails stuck into the potatoes.

This is beginning to sound like the old song "There's a frog on a bump on a log in the hole in the bottom of the sea," isn't it? But round up the ingredients from the kitchen, the toolbox, and maybe the bedside table, and see what it's all about. It's about time you got started, isn't it?

YOU WILL NEED

- A basic, low-voltage LED clock (which uses a 1- to 2-volt button-type battery)
- 2 galvanized nails (it's important to be sure they're galvanized, so ask)
- 2 potatoes
- 2 three-inch (8 cm) lengths of copper wire
- 3 alligator clip wire units (short lengths of coated wire with alligator clips at each end)

METHOD

1 Remove the battery from the clock.

Insert a nail into each potato.

Insert a length of copper wire into each potato (as far from the nail as possible).

Use an alligator clip to connect the copper wire of one potato to the positive (+) terminal of the clock's battery compartment.

Use another alligator clip to connect the nail of the other potato to the negative (-) battery terminal.

Use the third clip to connect the nail of potato 1 to the wire of potato 2.

Set the clock. It should now be running.

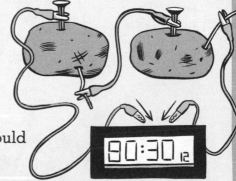

HEY, WHAT'S GOING ON?

The potato acted as an electrochemical cell—that is, a cell where chemical energy is converted into electrical energy. The zinc (in the nail) reacts with the copper of the wire. The potato contains phosphoric acid, which reacts with the zinc and releases electrons from the zinc. Zinc atoms that have lost (negatively charged) electrons become positively charged ions. (Remember that ions are atoms or molecules with a positive or negative charge because they've lost or gained electrons.) The potato conducts electrons but keeps the zinc ions separate from the copper ions. That means that the electrons in the copper are forced to move (forming an electrical current). And it's that current that powers the clock.

ATOMIC NUMBER: 50	ELECTRONS IN OUTERMOST SHELL: 4
ATOMIC WEIGHT: 118.710	MELTING POINT: 449.47°F (231.93°C)
ELEMENT SYMBOL: Sn	BOILING POINT: 4,716°F (2,602°C)

CHAPTER 20

1 H																	2 He
3 Li	4 Be											5 B	6 C	7 N	8 O	9 F	10 Ne
11 Na	12 Mg											13 Al	14 Si	15 P	16 S	17 Cl	18 Ar
19 K	20 Ca	21 Sc	22 Ti	23 V	24 Cr	25 Mn	26 Fe	27 Co	28 Ni	29 Cu	30 Zn	31 Ga	32 Ge	33 As	34 Se	35 Br	36 Kr
37 Rb	38 Sr	39 Y	40 Zr	41 Nb	42 Mo	43 Tc	44 Ru	45 Rh	46 Pd	47 Ag	48 Cd	49 In	50 Sn	51 Sb	52 Te	53 I	54 Xe
55 Cs	56 Ba		72 Hf	73 Ta	74 W	75 Re	76 Os	77 Ir	78 Pt	79 Au	80 Hg	81 Tl	82 Pb	83 Bi	84 Po	85 At	86 Rn
87 Fr	88 Ra		104 Rf	105 Db	106 Sg	107 Bh	108 Hs	109 Mt	110 Ds	111 Rg	112 Cn	113 Nh	114 Fl	115 Mc	116 Lv	117 Ts	118 Og

57 La	58 Ce	59 Pr	60 Nd	61 Pm	62 Sm	63 Eu	64 Gd	65 Tb	66 Dy	67 Ho	68 Er	69 Tm	70 Yb	71 Lu
89 Ac	90 Th	91 Pa	92 U	93 Np	94 Pu	95 Am	96 Cm	97 Bk	98 Cf	99 Es	100 Fm	101 Md	102 No	103 Lr

I f ever an element could be described as a "team player," it would have to be tin. On its own, it's a humble metal — a little too weak and bendable to match more powerful workhorses such as iron and aluminum. But some of those other, stronger metals have weaknesses of their own, like their tendency to rust or tarnish. And where do metalworkers turn to give those metals a protective layer? That's right, to humble old tin.

But tin isn't important just as a coating. It's a great alloy ingredient, as well. In fact, one of the most important periods in human history takes its name from the alloy that tin forms with copper. The Bronze Age, beginning about 5,600 years ago, marked the breakthrough period when humans moved from the more primitive Stone Age into new civilizations with writing and complex societies. Tin to the rescue again!

WHAT DOES TIN LOOK LIKE?

Pure tin is a silver-white solid at room temperature. It is malleable (easily bent into shape) and ductile (easily formed into wire). Unlike many metals, tin does not rust on contact with the air. That quality, coupled with its softness, makes it useful as a protective coating over other metals.

Something odd happens to tin when temperatures dip to about 55°F (14°C). The solid, silvery metal begins to turn gray. Colder still, down to about 14°F (-10°C), it turns into a gray powder or dust. That's because the tin rearranges itself into a new allotrope (see page 136) at these lower temperatures. This new form of tin is called "tin pest" or "tin plague." You can see why people would be pretty negative about it when you learn how they first noticed the change (see "Danger Level," page 204).

All of this applies, of course, to tin on its own. But tin really shines (in more ways than one) when it's coupled with copper to become golden-brown bronze—an alloy that's much stronger than its two metal ingredients.

WHEN WAS TIN DISCOVERED?

Jewelry and household items found in Egyptian tombs indicate that people used tin on its own at least 4,000 years ago. It's fascinating that we can find objects made of bronze (the copper–tin alloy) more than 1,500 years older than that too, though. Quite separately, people in different parts of the world (the Middle East, India, and China) began developing bronze between 5,000 and 5,600 years ago.

This breakthrough—coming up with an alloy that could be formed into all sorts of shapes while still being harder than its two ingredients—coincided with huge advances in human civilizations. Could it be that the new metal made hunting and farming easier, so people had more time to develop writing, building skills, and religious beliefs? Or perhaps bronze weapons allowed some societies to defeat their neighbors and *that* gave the conquerors the free time to develop? Whatever the exact reason, it was that 5 percent addition of tin to 95 percent copper that triggered the arrival of the Bronze Age.

WHERE IS TIN USED?

Apart from its many uses in the alloy bronze, tin is a versatile element. It also forms alloys with other metals, notably as pewter.

On its own, tin is used to coat other metals to protect them from corrosion and other chemical reactions. "Tin cans," for example, are really made of steel with a protective coating of tin.

Window glass, when it is still molten, is often floated on top of molten tin to produce a flat surface.

For a while in the 1950s, tin was bonded with the element fluoride to make more effective toothpastes. The resulting compound, stannous fluoride, helped prevent cavities. ("Stannous" means "relating to tin"—think of tin's symbol, Sn.) When many people complained of a metallic taste and a gritty feel to the toothpaste, stannous fluoride was replaced with better-tasting sodium fluoride. Some dentists still prefer the "tin version" because it's better at neutralizing tooth-eating acid produced by microbes in the mouth.

MICROBE

Microbes are tiny one-celled organisms that are the oldest form of life on Earth. They are everywhere: You'd find more on your hand than there are people on the planet. Some microbes can help the body with many jobs, while others cause harmful diseases.

DANGER LEVEL

☢ ☢ ☢ ☢ ☢

Tin is completely safe to handle, but let's get back to that allotropic stuff. "Tin pest" sounds like something a bit annoying that you could still deal with easily—like a mild sunburn, or a mosquito bite, or your little brother or sister in a robot costume. It was first noted in European church organs. Many of those organs have tin pipes, and many of the churches in northern Europe get pretty chilly inside. When organists began to notice the pipes of their instruments crumbling and falling apart each winter, they figured that it was the fault of the Devil.

The other term—"tin plague"—is a better description of a more recent and deadly example of tin's allotropic change. In the winter of 1812, Napoleon Bonaparte led the remains of his 500,000 French Imperial soldiers on a retreat from Russia. Temperatures reached -40°F (-40°C), and only about 30,000 French soldiers eventually made it home. Reports blamed tin pest for some of these deaths—the French uniforms had tin buttons, which would have lost their strength at those temperatures, leaving the coats flapping open in the freezing Russian winter wind.

TELLURIUM: DRACULA'S CURSE?

1 H																	2 He
3 Li	4 Be											5 B	6 C	7 N	8 O	9 F	10 Ne
11 Na	12 Mg											13 Al	14 Si	15 P	16 S	17 Cl	18 Ar
19 K	20 Ca	21 Sc	22 Ti	23 V	24 Cr	25 Mn	26 Fe	27 Co	28 Ni	29 Cu	30 Zn	31 Ga	32 Ge	33 As	34 Se	35 Br	36 Kr
37 Rb	38 Sr	39 Y	40 Zr	41 Nb	42 Mo	43 Tc	44 Ru	45 Rh	46 Pd	47 Ag	48 Cd	49 In	50 Sn	51 Sb	52 Te	53 I	54 Xe
55 Cs	56 Ba		72 Hf	73 Ta	74 W	75 Re	76 Os	77 Ir	78 Pt	79 Au	80 Hg	81 Tl	82 Pb	83 Bi	84 Po	85 At	86 Rn
87 Fr	88 Ra		104 Rf	105 Db	106 Sg	107 Bh	108 Hs	109 Mt	110 Ds	111 Rg	112 Cn	113 Nh	114 Fl	115 Mc	116 Lv	117 Ts	118 Og

57 La	58 Ce	59 Pr	60 Nd	61 Pm	62 Sm	63 Eu	64 Gd	65 Tb	66 Dy	67 Ho	68 Er	69 Tm	70 Yb	71 Lu
89 Ac	90 Th	91 Pa	92 U	93 Np	94 Pu	95 Am	96 Cm	97 Bk	98 Cf	99 Es	100 Fm	101 Md	102 No	103 Lr

Look two elements to the right of tin, along period 5 of the periodic table, and there lies the element tellurium (Te). This rare metalloid element does have a few uses in industry, either alloyed with lead or in making artificial rubber. Plus, it crops up in CD and DVD production. But go anywhere near it, and you'll pick up a horrible smell of garlic, the bane of any vampire's existence. It just so happens that this mysterious element was first identified in 1783 in Transylvania—Dracula's neck of the woods!

EXPERIMENT *with the* ELEMENT

The next experiment is a quick, hands-on examination of one way that we come across tin every day. You should be able to see exactly why it's so useful and what life would have been like before we used it this way.

IS THAT A TIN "TIN CAN"?

This simple experiment is going to call for an empty can, or more than one, if you choose the wrong one the first time around. Hopefully you have a choice of empty cans waiting to be recycled. But before that can gets recycled, it has another job to do. It will help you understand the properties of different metals and show you how some of them produce a chemical reaction when combined with something very ordinary—water.

YOU WILL NEED

- **Empty can (that once held fruit or vegetables)**
- **Refrigerator magnet**
- **Sandpaper**

WARNING! Be careful handling the sharp rims of empty cans.

METHOD

1 First, check that you have a steel-based can by using a refrigerator magnet. If the can sticks to it, then it's steel. If not, then it's aluminum, and you need to find a different one.

2 Peel the paper off the can.

3   Use sandpaper to rub the surface of part of the can (about the size of four postage stamps). Rub until you see a different color beneath.

4   Run the can under the faucet for about 10 seconds and leave it alone for several days.

5   Check to see which area has rusted.

HEY, WHAT'S GOING ON?

This is a good way to find out what "tin" cans are really made from. Once you determined that the can wasn't aluminum by using the magnet, you knew that you had a steel can. The bit that you rubbed off was the thin layer of protective tin that these cans have. Tin doesn't oxidize (rust) when exposed to oxygen and moisture, so it protects the metal inside it. And by the end, you'll see what that protective layer is protecting the steel can from.

BONUS ACTIVITY:
BECAUSE YOU'RE WORTH IT

By now you should be familiar with lots of the ways that elements present themselves, how they behave, and how they react with each other to create . . . well, to create EVERYTHING. You also know that you're made up of a combination of these elements, and that we can work out how much you'd have to pay for a certain amount of each element.

Sooo, you can work out how much you're worth in elements. That's what this experiment (or demonstration) is all about. How do you do it? Well, first of all, you should do what scientists do and work in the metric system. That means converting your weight into kilograms. To do that, use a calculator to divide your weight in pounds by 2.208.

Below you'll see the top 12 elements in terms of what proportion of your body mass (your weight in kilograms) they make up. You can work out how many kilos of your body's total is made up of each element. Next you'll see the typical cost (per kilo) of each element. It's not exact, but it's a good ballpark figure. From there you can work out the value of each element and the overall total.

To make life easy, we've worked it all out for a kid weighing 35 kilograms (kg). You can use the same math to work out your own value.

ELEMENT	% OF BODY MASS FROM THE ELEMENT	MASS OF ELEMENT IN A 35 KG CHILD	PRICE PER KG ($/KG)	VALUE OF ELEMENT IN 35 KG CHILD
OXYGEN	61	21.4 kg	$3.00	$64.20
CARBON	23	8 kg	$24.00	$192.00
HYDROGEN	10	3.5 kg	$5.00	$17.50
NITROGEN	2.5	900 g	$5.00	$4.50
CALCIUM	1.4	500 g	$200.00	$100.00
PHOSPHORUS	0.55	385 g	$300.00	$115.50
POTASSIUM	0.2	70 g	$1000.00	$70.00
SULFUR	0.2	70 g	$500.00	$35.00
SODIUM	0.14	49 g	$250.00	$12.25
CHLORINE	0.13	47 g	$1.50	$0.07
MANGANESE	0.03	11 g	$1.50	$0.02
IRON	0.006	2.1 g	$72.00	$0.15
			TOTAL	**$611.19**

Are you worth more or less than that?

THE "DIRTY DOZEN"

This book finishes off with snapshots of some really deadly elements. Some of them could blow the world up right now—in an instant. Others were once thought harmless, or even helpful, until scientists learned more about their horrible effects. And just as some of the 20 "hands-on" elements had dangerous side effects, some of the "Dirty Dozen" can be tamed and turned to our own benefit.

It's a funny old world!

33	ATOMIC NUMBER: 33	ELECTRONS IN OUTERMOST SHELL: 5
As	ATOMIC WEIGHT: 74.9216	MELTING POINT: 1,503°F (817°C)
	ELEMENT SYMBOL: As	BOILING POINT: 1,137°F (614°C)

Arsenic is a heavy metal that was once the most popular form of poison for murderers. Or at least that's how it seems if you read lots of murder mysteries from the 19th century. Some arsenic would be slipped into someone's food, or a cup of tea, and within an hour or so, Sherlock Holmes or some other investigator would be called in to solve the mystery of the corpse at the dinner table.

It's true that arsenic is deadly. The good news is that it's harder to get hold of nowadays than it was 150 years ago. Pure arsenic is also less poisonous than arsenic in compound form. That's because the body doesn't really absorb arsenic and instead sends it away in urine. The bad news is that it's still possible to come across arsenic in some of its compounds with other elements. And it's the body's need for those elements (such as hydrogen and oxygen) that allows arsenic to sneak in.

Arsenic is unusual among chemical elements because it sublimates. That means that when heated, solid arsenic becomes a gas without becoming a liquid along the way. Arsenic compounds have many uses, ranging from wood preservatives to strengthening metal alloys. One compound, gallium arsenide, is used in the electronics industry. It can convert electric current into laser light.

NAPOLEON'S DEMISE?

Some scientists believe that Napoleon Bonaparte died of arsenic poisoning in 1821. He had been sent to the island prison of St. Helena in the South Atlantic Ocean, so it seems unlikely that a political enemy could have traveled that distance to kill him. Two bits of evidence suggest that it might have been accidental arsenic poisoning. The first is that studies show a large amount of arsenic in Napoleon's hair. The second is that arsenic was often used in paints for wallpaper — of the sort that was in Napoleon's room. He might simply have breathed it in over a long period.

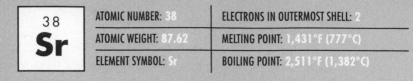

38 Sr	ATOMIC NUMBER: 38	ELECTRONS IN OUTERMOST SHELL: 2
	ATOMIC WEIGHT: 87.62	MELTING POINT: 1,431°F (777°C)
	ELEMENT SYMBOL: Sr	BOILING POINT: 2,511°F (1,382°C)

STRONTIUM

Strontium takes its name from the Scottish town of Strontian, where it was first identified as an element in 1790. And if it weren't for one feature of one particular variation (isotope) of this element, we'd consider it to embody all the best Scottish qualities, like reliability and industriousness. It has some important industrial applications, and is used to make glass for television sets, produce magnets, and refine zinc.

To get an idea of why it poses such danger, check out its position on the periodic table. Right above it in group 2 is calcium. We know that calcium is vital for our bones and for our bodies in general. Well, strontium behaves a lot like calcium and given half a chance will compete with it to form bonds. So, it's this calcium-strontium-bone connection that's the key to the trouble.

It all boils down to neutrons. Elements are defined by the number of protons they have, usually balanced by a similar amount of electrons. But they can have different numbers of neutrons. These neutron particles have no charge, but they do have about the same mass as protons. Each variation of an atom (with more or fewer neutrons) is called an isotope, and we name isotopes by giving them the element name followed by the total of protons and neutrons.

That sounds complicated but it's not. Strontium has four naturally occurring isotopes: Sr-84, Sr-86, Sr-87, and Sr-88. You can work out how many neutrons each has by subtracting the number of protons (38), which is the same in each case. So these four isotopes have 46, 48, 49, and 50 neutrons.

The real problem is with Sr-90, which is produced as a result of nuclear fission (splitting atoms for power or weapons). It carries dangerous radiation, and we can absorb it from the air or from contaminated food or drink, such as milk. And because strontium mimics calcium, this dangerous isotope can enter our very bones. That's where it is very dangerous, destroying bone marrow and causing cancer. Steer clear!

CADMIUM

It can't be too glorious for an element to be thought of as an impurity while isolating another element, but that's what happened with cadmium. We know it as an element in its own right (sitting below zinc in the periodic table), though it first appeared by accident in 1817 as German scientists were working with a zinc compound called zinc carbonate.

Since it's in the same group as zinc, cadmium shares a lot of qualities with its neighbor, but it's much rarer and has fewer obvious uses. It can strengthen copper without reducing copper's usefulness as an electrical conductor. Along with nickel, cadmium is also used in rechargeable batteries.

You can imagine workers in factories and workshops handling this rather dull, reasonably useful material on a daily basis as they went about their business plating things or assembling batteries. But every day they were absorbing small amounts of the cadmium. Although the amounts were tiny, they accumulated inside the body, which couldn't get rid of it. We now know that this cadmium buildup was increasing each worker's risk of being poisoned, and even worse, of passing on the results of that poisoning to children.

Even in small doses, cadmium damages the body's ability to defend itself. A small amount would produce what's called "cadmium blues"—flu-like symptoms of aches and chills. Cadmium can go further, especially if it is inhaled, by damaging various organs or triggering cancer.

QUICK RECALL

Companies need to act quickly if they believe they are exposing the public to the risks of cadmium. For example, cadmium was detected in the paint used for some promotional drinking glasses displayed in McDonald's restaurants in June 2010. The company took this very seriously and set up an immediate recall of the glasses—all 12 million of them!

ATOMIC NUMBER: 55	ELECTRONS IN OUTERMOST SHELL: 1
ATOMIC WEIGHT: 132.9054	MELTING POINT: 83.3°F (28.5°C)
ELEMENT SYMBOL: Cs	BOILING POINT: 1,240°F (671°C)

55
Cs

CESIUM

esium, an otherwise low-profile element, played an important part in the worst nuclear power disaster in history. On April 26, 1986, workers were carrying out routine tests on a nuclear reactor at the Chernobyl power plant near the city of Pripyat, Ukraine. An unexpected power surge damaged part of the plant and triggered a destructive fire. A disaster was under way. There was a full-blown meltdown, and the town was evacuated!

The fire sent a plume of radioactive material high into the air, and this cloud began to drift across much of Eastern Europe. As well as containing the strontium isotope Sr-90 (see page 215), it had alarmingly high levels of a deadly isotope of the element cesium. This isotope, Cs-17, doesn't necessarily have more radiation than Sr-90 or some of the other strontium isotopes. It does, however, pose real dangers because it is cesium.

Sure, cesium isn't really toxic, in the sense that you're not going to die from touching it. (Either way, better play it safe and leave that cesium alone!) But think of where cesium sits on the periodic table, in group 1. And think of just how reactive those other alkali elements are (sodium and potassium, for starters). Well, cesium is also trying to get rid of its extra valence electron, so it forms compounds very easily, and that's the start of the problem.

Now imagine a version of cesium that has all of its reactive nature . . . plus a potentially deadly dose of radiation. That's what you have with Cs-17. Just as other elements in its group produce salts (think of sodium chloride), cesium forms many compounds that dissolve in water. That, in turn, means that they are absorbed by plants, which are eaten by animals, which in turn are eaten by humans. And so, the deadly cesium isotope can make its way into humans.

80 Hg		
ATOMIC NUMBER: 80		ELECTRONS IN OUTERMOST SHELL: 1
ATOMIC WEIGHT: 15.9994		MELTING POINT: -37.89°F (-38.83°C)
ELEMENT SYMBOL: Hg		BOILING POINT: 674.11°F (356.73°C)

MERCURY

Mercury, named for the quick-footed messenger of the Roman gods, has intrigued humans for thousands of years. It's the only common metal that is liquid at room temperature. A liquid metal? That's pretty cool. And sure enough, mercury has built up a legendary reputation over time, from the earliest examples (it has been found in 3,500-year-old Egyptian tombs, and Chinese emperors thought it would prolong their lives), through the Middle Ages, and into the modern scientific period.

Even the mysterious alchemists (see page 137) were in on the act. Many of them believed that it was the most important substance on Earth, and that its combined solid-liquid nature would help them find the link between ordinary metals and gold. They never did find that missing link, but they helped stoke interest in this mysterious element.

Spill mercury and it turns into funny little shiny balls. Roll them back together, and they form a liquid again. There seemed to be no end to the amusing spin-offs of this magical metal. And then scientists found practical uses for mercury: It responds very dramatically to changes in temperature and air pressure, which made it ideal in weather instruments such as thermometers and barometers. Plus, mercury can help extract other precious metals from their ores.

Something that has mystical qualities, looks cool, is fun to play with, and has some pretty good uses—what's not to like about an element like that?

Well, sorry to be a party pooper, but mercury is poisonous. German chemist Alfred Stock first announced the bad news in 1926 after witnessing poisoning among his fellow scientists who worked with it. (Mercury had been used in many medical and dental treatments.) After this announcement, the "charge sheet" against mercury grew longer and longer.

Mercury poisoning harms the brain, heart, kidneys, lungs, and immune systems of affected people. We now know that our bodies can absorb mercury through the air and through what we eat, especially some types of fish. Those foods are constantly checked for mercury so that what we buy is safe.

LEAD

Like mercury, lead is an element that misled people for a long, long time before they understood its dangers. We're talking here not of an element that was a rich child's toy, or in an alchemist's bottle, or sealed up in the glass tubes of thermometers like mercury, but an element that seemed to be all over the place. It was everywhere for millennia.

Imagine a metal that is easily mined and smelted, can be hammered or bent into shape, and resists corrosion. These qualities made it an obvious choice for all sorts of purposes, but probably the most important of these was in plumbing.

"Bends into shape? Won't rust? Doesn't cost an awful lot? Yep—I think we have the ideal metal for all the plumbing in the Roman Empire. It's lead!"

Sure enough, the Romans were the ones who really put lead on the map. Take a look at the symbol for lead—Pb. That's an abbreviation for the Latin word for lead, *plumbum*. That doesn't sound much like our word "lead," does it? But it does sound a lot like "plumber." So you can see that the Romans weren't the only ones to work with lead. And people didn't stop with pipes. Lead wound up in paints, cables, roofs, and even in gasoline (where it's sent out in the exhaust).

OK. Where's the catch? Three guesses. Right, right, and right—it's poisonous. Lead is dangerous, whether it's inhaled (think of those traffic jams) or swallowed. Lead is also a cumulative poison, meaning that it builds up inside the system. That makes it especially dangerous for young children, because their growing bodies are geared to absorbing substances.

Lead travels through the body in the bloodstream, where it limits the blood's ability to carry oxygen. That leaves people weak with a condition called anemia. It causes more problems when it reaches the bones: It affects the marrow, where blood cells are made, and it interferes with the way that the body absorbs calcium (see page 163).

POLONIUM

On November 1, 2006, Alexander Litvinenko became suddenly ill and was rushed to a hospital in London. Litvinenko was a former Russian security agent who had fled to Britain, and he had many enemies back in Russia. Litvinenko never left the hospital alive. His condition worsened by the hour. The Russian's hair fell out and he could no longer walk. Finally, on November 26, he died.

Medical scientists concluded that the cause of death was an isotope of the element polonium, Po-210. Litvinenko's body contained five times the dose of polonium that would kill someone. The circumstances certainly were suspicious, given Litvinenko's mysterious past.

Polonium could hit you with what sports reporters used to call the "double whammy." It could kill you outright with its chemical properties alone (like arsenic), but if that didn't do the trick, it would get you with radiation. And it's the radiation side of Po-210 that killed Litvinenko. Po-210 emits radiation through alpha particles. These particles are harder to detect than the gamma particles that other elements emit because alpha particles don't travel as far as gamma particles. Alpha particles can't penetrate the skin, so Po-210 is harmless outside your body unless you inhale it. Or, as in the case of the Litvinenko death, swallow it.

Once inside the body, though, the alpha particles can destroy the genetic "machinery" of the body's cells. With this genetic short-circuit, some cells mutate (change form) and grow into cancerous tumors. Some studies, dating back to the early 1960s, have detected Po-210 in tobacco smoke. Considering that many smokers develop lung cancer, it's possible that polonium plays a part.

RADON

Whoa—wait a minute!! Eight electrons in the outer shell! What's a noble gas like radon doing in with these other elements? Surely there's been a mistake. Those noble elements are harmless, right? They never bother any other elements, do they? No big explosions in water. No corrosion when they form compounds—because they *don't* form compounds. What's going on here?

Well, the truth is, you don't necessarily need a second element, or a chemical reaction, to send out a danger signal. It's what the element does on its own that puts it in the "high risk" category. And with some of the elements at the very bottom of the periodic table, that risk comes from radiation. Some of these elements are unstable, which means that they break down and "radiate" (send out) energy in the form of alpha, beta, and gamma rays. New elements then form, but *they* might be unstable and begin to emit energy . . . and so on, until a stable element forms.

Radon appears in the middle of this process. It forms from the decay of radium and naturally occurring uranium (see page 232) in rocks and soil around the world. It emits alpha rays, just as polonium does (see page 224), so you can understand how dangerous it can be.

Despite that link with deadly radiation, radon could also be compared to mercury and lead. Each of these were in use for years and considered harmless until their dangers were recognized. Radon could take that a step further. It wasn't just used—for a while just over a century ago, it was even touted as promoting health and well-being. That's because radon gas dissolves in water— just as people detected it in Hot Springs, Arkansas. Natural hot springs often do contain soothing or helpful minerals in them, and that's partly why European cities with names like Spa (Belgium) and Bath (England) developed.

Finding a radioactive element in a hot spring was bad news for bathers, but the discovery wasn't all bad. It showed the public how radon could be present in the unlikeliest of places, so people started looking for it to be safe. Sure enough, radon detectors find traces of it in homes, schools, and other public places. Luckily we have methods of reducing radon exposure with improved ventilation, better sealants around doors and windows, and more efficient drainage. OK, it's bath time!

87 Fr	ATOMIC NUMBER: 87	ELECTRONS IN OUTERMOST SHELL: 1
	ATOMIC WEIGHT: 223	MELTING POINT: 80°F (26.6°C)
	ELEMENT SYMBOL: Fr	BOILING POINT: 1,250°F (677°C)

FRANCIUM

Can you guess where francium was discovered in 1939? That's right, the element's discoverer, Marguerite Perey, named the new element for her home country of France. (Interestingly, there's another element—gallium—named for France, except that's the country's old name, Gaul.) The identification of the new element was another pat on the back for Dmitri Mendeleev, who was convinced that there had to be another element beneath cesium in column 1 of his periodic table. He even called the yet-to-be-discovered element eka-cesium, using the ancient Indian language Sanskrit to name it "the one after cesium."

Francium's discovery marked a milestone in scientific history: It is the last naturally occurring element to have been discovered and identified. Every element that has been noted since then (the "synthetic elements") has been the result of experiments involving powerful nuclear equipment, and some of those elements last only for a split second before they start decaying.

HALF-LIFE

Radioactive elements—those that decay by sending out alpha, beta, and gamma rays—break down at steady rates. Scientists measure the rate by describing the element's half-life, or the amount of time it takes for half of the atoms in a sample of an element to decay. The longest half-life is measured in billions of years; the shortest takes only a tiny fraction of a second.

While francium does occur naturally, it's super-rare because it, too, decays and has a half-life of only 22 minutes. In fact, it's the rarest naturally occurring element in the Earth's crust. Scientists estimate that there's only about one ounce of francium on the planet at any one time. (So if you find some, make sure to tell your science teacher!)

All of this leads to a funny conclusion, and maybe you'll feel relieved: As you scroll down group 1 of the periodic table (the alkali group), you see that the elements become more and more reactive—they produce bigger and bigger results. Francium, right at the bottom, would no doubt produce the biggest boom of all, but because it's so radioactive (always decaying), we will never see such a reaction. So you can thank radioactivity for at least one development.

88	ATOMIC NUMBER: 88	ELECTRONS IN OUTERMOST SHELL: 2
Ra	ATOMIC WEIGHT: 226	MELTING POINT: 1,292°F (700°C)
	ELEMENT SYMBOL: Ra	BOILING POINT: 3,159°F (1,737°C)

RADIUM

Hmmm. Radium. Radioactive. Radiation . . . This is going to be trouble, isn't it? We know nowadays that it will be, but that wasn't always the case. In fact, when radium first became widely known, it was seen as a medicine and a miraculous way of making clocks and watches visible in the dark.

In 1923, a New Jersey bank teller named Grace Fryer went to her dentist complaining of a bad pain in her jaw. The dentist was shocked when he examined her: Grace's jaw had been badly damaged and looked more like a sponge than a solid bone. But Grace wasn't the only young woman in that area to display those symptoms. Soon it became clear that all of those women—with their falling-out teeth and handkerchiefs that glowed when they blew their noses—had one thing in common. They had all worked in the same factory, painting dials on watches and clocks.

And it wasn't any old paint that the women had used. It was a glow-in-the-dark paint made with an exciting new ingredient: the element radium. As radium decays, it emits energy, causing the electrons in nearby elements—such as the zinc–sulfur compound coating the clock and watch dials—to become active and produce light. As the women painted the clocks at the U.S. Radium Corporation factory, they would put their paintbrushes to their lips to get a finer point. There was no funny taste, and there's no way they could have sensed harm. But the women were taking in dangerous levels of a radioactive element. In the following years, they all began to face severe health problems.

By the mid-1920s, the famous New York journalist and newspaper editor Walter Lippmann publicized their case. The "Radium Girls" took their former company to court and eventually won. Their experience helped change work practices in the United States and beyond, as companies had to pay more attention to the risks that their workers faced.

Modern regulations strictly limit the use of radium and make sure that workers can claim compensation for illnesses that develop from their labor.

URANIUM

On August 6, 1945, a USAF B-29 bomber, the *Enola Gay*, took off from an airfield in the Pacific Ocean. After a six-hour flight, it reached its destination—Japan. The United States and Japan had been at war for nearly four years. Although the Japanese forces had been pushed back to their home country—and despite the fact that Japan's ally, Germany, had surrendered in early May—the Japanese government refused to surrender. The *Enola Gay*'s flight, and a similar one three days later, would change all that.

The *Enola Gay* was carrying a deadly new type of weapon, an atomic bomb that used the properties of uranium to release vast amounts of energy. Uranium is fissile, which means that it can be part of a chain reaction (that's the bit that releases all the energy). A chain reaction is a complicated process, but at its heart it is relatively easy to explain.

If a neutron is fired into some fissile material, the atom it hits will split apart. That's where all the energy that holds the atom together is released. But there's more—as the atom splits, it releases two neutrons. And each of *them* flies off to split two more atoms. And then each of *those* atoms split two more atoms . . . Now you can see where the term "chain reaction" comes from.

The bomb dropped on August 6 was devastating. Code-named "Little Boy" by the military, it exploded 2,000 feet over the city of Hiroshima. Almost everything within a mile of the point of the explosion was wiped out. About 75,000 people died in the blast and a similar number were injured. And the most shocking aspect of the explosion is that it wasn't very efficient: Only 1.7 percent of the uranium in the bomb actually split apart.

The Hiroshima explosion announced the arrival of a devastating new type of weapon harnessing the atomic potential of uranium and other elements. But that same power can be turned to peaceful purposes. Some scientists claim that the cleanest, most efficient way of producing energy for civilian use is to harness those same forces. Others, remembering Hiroshima and the emergencies at Chernobyl (see page 218) and other power stations, want no part of that future.

94	ATOMIC NUMBER: 94
Pu	ATOMIC WEIGHT: 244
	ELEMENT SYMBOL: Pu

ELECTRONS IN OUTERMOST SHELL: 2
MELTING POINT: 1,182.9°F (639.4°C)
BOILING POINT: 5,842°F (3,228°C)

PLUTONIUM

P lutonium is one of the "synthetic elements" at the bottom of the periodic table. It was first isolated in 1940 after Glenn Saborg and other scientists in Berkeley, California, bombarded an isotope of uranium with particles. Naming the new element was pretty simple. Element number 92 is uranium, and number 93 is neptunium; Uranus is the seventh planet in our solar system and Neptune is the eighth. And in 1930, scientists had added a ninth planet, Pluto, to the solar system . . . so element 94 nearly named itself. (In 2006, astronomers downgraded Pluto to a new category of "dwarf planet," but the element's name has stuck.)

Even before plutonium's discovery, many people could predict how such a new element would be put to use. In 1939, while Europe had already entered World War II, a number of scientists (including Albert Einstein) signed a letter addressed to President Franklin Roosevelt. They informed him of a possible new type of weapon (nuclear weapons) and warned him that Germany and its allies would be trying to produce such weapons.

By 1942 (with the United States now in the war), the government had set up the top-secret Manhattan Project, designed to develop nuclear weapons. Two types of fuel were possible—uranium and the new element, plutonium. Of the two, plutonium was considered more efficient. A plutonium bomb was tested in the New Mexico desert on July 16, 1945. This event—rather than the Hiroshima bombing (see page 233)—marked the real dawn of the Atomic Age, because up until then, no one could be absolutely sure about the power of an atomic explosion.

On the day of the test, scientists and high-ranking military personnel gathered at an observation tower 10 miles from the test site. Some of the scientists even bet each other about whether the test would be a dud, a controlled success, or if an unstoppable reaction would burn up the atmosphere. It turned out exactly as planned, producing an intense light, an enormous explosion, and a mushroom-shaped cloud. A blind woman living 150 miles away was quoted as asking, "What's that brilliant light?"

Back at the observation tower, observers felt a mixture of relief and anxiety. They knew that they had a weapon that could help end the war, but they also knew that the destructive power that they had unleashed could one day have devastating consequences.

J. Robert Oppenheimer, director of the Manhattan Project, later said that two lines from sacred Hindu texts came to him as he witnessed the successful test. They sum up both the potential and danger of the power that plutonium had unleashed:

"If the radiance of a thousand suns were to burst at once into the sky, that would be like the splendor of the mighty one."

"I am become Death, destroyer of worlds."

GLOSSARY

ACID: A chemical substance (often corrosive) that combines with a base to form a salt.

ALKALINE: Having the properties of a base and capable of neutralizing some acids.

ALLOTROPE: Any one of the different forms that some elements can bond themselves into (coal and diamonds are allotropes of carbon).

ALLOY: A metal made by melting and mixing together two or more other metals.

ANTIMATTER: Matter made up of antiparticles (subatomic particles that have the opposite charge to protons and electrons).

ATMOSPHERE: The layer of gases surrounding the Earth and other planets.

ATOM: A substance composed of one type of element, which cannot be broken down into anything smaller without losing its essential qualities.

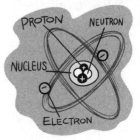

ATOMIC NUMBER: The number of protons in the nucleus of an atom, determining its place in the periodic table.

ATOMIC WEIGHT: The mass of one atom of an element.

BASE: A chemical compound (often corrosive) that combines with an acid to form a salt.

BIG BANG: A theoretical event about 14 billion years ago during which a small amount of matter exploded and expanded to create the universe.

BOILING POINT: The temperature at which something boils.

BOND: A force that holds together atoms, ions, molecules, and other chemical substances.

CHEMICAL SYMBOL: One or two letters that stand for an element.

COMBUSTION: The process of a substance reacting with oxygen to produce heat and light, such as burning.

COMPOUND: A substance containing two or more elements.

CONDUCTOR: A material that transfers heat, sound, electricity, light, or any other form of energy.

CONTROL: Sometimes called the control variable, an object that stays constant during an experiment and is used to compare or measure change on other substances during the experiment.

CORRODE: To damage or destroy through slow chemical action. Substances that can corrode others are called corrosive.

COVALENT: A type of bond formed when two or more atoms share electrons to make a molecule.

CRYSTAL: A solid material formed from a regular pattern of atoms or molecules.

DISSOLVE (OF A SOLID): To become incorporated into a liquid; the resulting liquid is called a solution.

DNA: An abbreviation of deoxyribonucleic acid, a material present in nearly all living things and carrying the genetic code ("chemical building blocks") of those living things.

ELECTRON: A subatomic particle with a negative charge.

ELECTRON SHELL: A layer of electrons orbiting the nucleus of an atom. (The first shell contains up to two electrons and every shell after that contains up to eight electrons.)

ELEMENT: Any of the more than 100 substances that cannot be broken down or changed into other substances by chemical reactions.

ENDOTHERMIC: Describing a chemical process that absorbs heat.

EXCITE (OF AN ELECTRON): To move into a different energy state.

EXOTHERMIC: Describing a chemical process that produces heat.

FLAMMABLE: A substance that catches fire readily.

FOSSIL FUEL: A source of energy (like coal or oil) that comes from fossilized plants; there is a limited supply of fossil fuel on Earth.

FRICTION: The force that resists, or acts against, the motion of one object against another.

GROUP: Elements that have the same number of electrons in their outer shell; each vertical column of the periodic table represents a group of elements.

HALF-LIFE: The amount of time it takes for half of the atoms of a particular element to decay.

HYDROPHILIC: Attracted to water.

HYPOTHESIS: A proposed explanation based on available evidence, used as a starting point for experiments.

INERT: Not producing a chemical reaction when combined with other elements.

ION: An atom or fragment of a molecule that has either a positive charge because of the loss of a negatively charged electron or a negative charge because it has gained an electron.

ISOTOPE: A version of an element that has more or fewer neutrons than it has protons.

LIQUID: A substance that has a constant volume but flows freely, like water from a pitcher.

MASS: A measure of how much matter is in an object. It is often measured by how much something weighs, but weight can change if there is a change in gravitational strength. A bowling ball would weigh less on the Moon (with its weaker gravity) than it would on Earth.

MATTER: Anything that occupies space and has mass. Energy is not matter because it has no mass and is not confined to space. But planets, books, sharks, and skis are all examples of matter.

MELTING POINT: The temperature at which something melts.

METAL: A substance that is strong and dense, solid at room temperature, and a good conductor of heat and electricity.

MOLECULE: A group of atoms that have joined together.

NEUTRALIZE: To cause an acid to lose its acidity by combining it in a chemical reaction with a base, or to cause a base to lose its alkalinity ("base-ness") by combining it with an acid. Such a neutralization always produces water and a salt.

NEUTRON: A neutrally charged subatomic particle that has about the same mass as a proton.

NOBLE ELEMENT: One of the seven elements that make up the farthest-right column (group 18) of the periodic table, all of which are highly resistant to chemical reaction.

NUCLEUS: The center of an atom; contains protons and often neutrons.

ORE: A mixture of elements containing one or more metals.

ORGANIC CHEMISTRY: A branch of chemistry that concentrates on studying matter containing carbon.

OXIDATION: A chemical reaction, such as rust, in which oxygen takes electrons from other materials, often changing their color and making them weaker.

PERIOD: A horizontal row on the periodic table containing elements that share the same number of electron shells.

PERIODIC TABLE: An array of chemical elements in an ascending order of atomic number so that horizontal rows indicate periods and columns represent groups.

PRISM: A glass or other transparent object that separates light into its spectrum of colors.

PROTON: A subatomic particle with a positive charge.

RADIATION: The sending out of energy, often in the form of moving subatomic particles. Some types of radiation, such as gamma rays, can be used medically to treat cancer and other diseases. But too much exposure to many types of radiation can change the structure of human cells, leading to illness and death.

RADIUS: The distance from the center of a circle or spinning object (like a nucleus) to the curve itself, or the surface of the spinning object.

REACTIVE: Able to undergo a chemical reaction, either by itself or by reacting with another substance.

SALT: A compound made up of two groups of oppositely charged ions. Usually the positive ions are from a metal and the negatively charged ions are from a nonmetal.

SCIENTIFIC METHOD: A method of research in which a problem is identified and data collected before a scientist makes a hypothesis. The hypothesis is then tested with practical observation, such as in an experiment.

SMELTING: Extracting metal from its ore by heating and melting.

SOLID: A substance that holds its shape and doesn't flow as a liquid does. An ice cube is simply water in its solid state of matter.

SOLUBLE: Able to dissolve into another substance. The substance that dissolves, like salt or sugar, is called a solute. The substance that it dissolves into (like water or coffee) is called a solvent. When a solute has dissolved into a solvent, the resulting mix is called a solution.

SPECTRUM: The broad range of visible light (colors ranging from red to violet) and other forms of radiation (such as gamma rays or infrared rays) that an object absorbs or sends out.

STABLE: Resistant to chemical change.

STATES OF MATTER: Often called "visible states of matter," the form in which humans observe matter—solid, liquid, gas, or plasma. Matter can change state when it is affected by a change in temperature, pressure, or electrical charge.

SUBATOMIC: Smaller than or occurring within an atom.

TARNISH: To lose a shiny surface because of a chemical reaction such as oxidation.

TRACE ELEMENT: An element, such as zinc or copper, that human bodies need in tiny amounts to perform specialized jobs in cells.

TRIPLE BOND: A chemical bond in which three pairs of electrons are share by two atoms. Triple bonds are extremely strong.

VALENCE ELECTRON: An electron on the outer shell of an atom. It is capable of forming bonds with other atoms.

X-RAY: A high-energy form of radiation that is able to pass through many materials that can block visible light.

GENIUS AT WORK!

More Books by
SEAN CONNOLLY

Sixty-four amazing science experiments that require no special training, use stuff from around the house, and demonstrate scientific principles like osmosis and Newton's Third Law of Motion.

Fifty awesome experiments that allow kids to understand 34 of the greatest scientific breakthroughs in history.

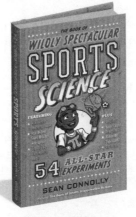

Math rocks! At least it does in the gifted hands of Sean Connolly, who blends middle school math with fantasy to create 24 problems that challenge readers on fractions, algebra, geometry, and more.

Fifty-four all-star experiments that demonstrate the scientific principles powering a variety of sports, from why a knuckleball flutters to how LeBron James seems to float through the air on a dunk.

The most infamous and dangerous disasters in the history of engineering come to life with 33 adrenaline-pumping experiments for daring young scientists.